Cross-Stitch Souvenirs

Cross-Stitch Souvenirs

40 PROJECTS FROM AROUND THE WORLD

Melinda Coss

COLLINS & BROWN

First published in Great Britain in 1997
by Collins & Brown Limited
London House
Great Eastern Wharf
Parkgate Road
London SW11 4NQ

1 3 5 7 9 8 6 4 2

British Library Cataloguing-in-Publication Data:
A catalogue record for this book
is available from the British Library.

ISBN 1 85585 281 0 (hardback edition)
ISBN 1 85585 405 8 (paperback edition)

Conceived, edited and designed by Collins & Brown Limited

Editor : Emma Callery
Designer: Roger Daniels
Photography: Jon Stewart

Reproduction by In-House Colour
Printed and bound in Italy by Arti Grafiche Bergamo

CONTENTS

INTRODUCTION

When I was a child, America was a place that visiting relatives returned from bringing gifts of multi-flavoured, multi-coloured chewing gum. These delicacies could only be bought in America and were treated as rare, exotic delights from a land where, in my mind, cowboys and Indians accounted for 99 per cent of the population. My mother, in contrast, was delighted by the gift of a beautiful patchwork quilt but, with a child's logic, I couldn't reason why anyone would want to cut up all that fabric simply to spend months stitching it back together again.

In later years, my own travels resulted in a collection of various souvenirs... castanets from Spain, boomerangs from Australia, tablecloths from Madeira, etc., etc. But, however humble the memento, each had a unique specialness because it 'belonged' to another place and could not be found at home.

The ease of travel has changed all this. Today, you can wander through any major city high street and find the very best of all the arts and crafts the world has to offer. Glorious hangings from India invite us to transform our homes into temples. Carpets from the Middle East add richness to any decor, and fabrics from France add that touch of elegance previously only dreamed of

by your average suburban house owner. With the added advantages of television and the Internet, you can travel the world in your armchair and be back in time to watch your favourite soap.

While this easy availability can be put to great use, the downside is that in a land of plenty we tend to forget, too quickly, the months of local labour and craftsmanship involved in producing a carpet or a hanging. Furthermore, the impact of unique patterns and

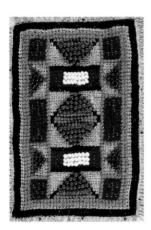

rich textures is somehow lost in the mire of commonplace.

This book is my attempt at bringing back the specialness of exotica. All the patterns and images that are now so easy for us to find can be used by you to create personal and unique cross-stitch items for your home. Many of the following patterns are inspired by historic embroidered fabrics which I have charted into designs that will fit comfortably in a contemporary landscape.

You, in turn, have the option of using the charts as you will. You can produce your own items from scratch or, with the use of waste canvas (see page 149), you can decorate existing table linen and soft furnishings using your choice of the motifs from the designs.

For beginners, we have a technique section that will talk you through the basics of cross stitch. Once you have mastered a single cross, no project in this book will be beyond your reach, although I would advise that your first project is worked on Aida fabric (see page 147) rather than on a finer fabric.

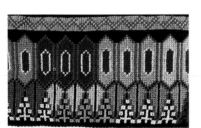

Unlike the women of Afghanistan, you have the opportunity of working traditional designs on a vast array of fabrics and the convenience of being able to pop down to the local high street for the odd skein of silk. We, in fact, are in the enviable position of having access to the best of everything and this can be reflected in our projects. Take an inspired design from Eastern Europe and re-create it with the best materials Western Europe or North America can offer... in other words, let's put it in a melting pot, stir it up and make it our own special treasure.

Enjoy your stitching.

NORTH AMERICAN
TRADITIONS

The craft traditions of native America stem from the need to make a comfortable home from very few resources. Here, I have used the popular images, but not the traditional techniques, of patchwork and Indian beadwork and translated them into what I hope will be useful and decorative projects. As you will see from my use of chamois leather, when working cross stitch you need not feel limited by traditional fabrics. A cross-stitch panel can be stitched or glued onto any material from silk to wood. So, decide what you want to make and then, when determining how to decorate it, just think cross stitch.

PATCHWORK BOX TOP

The theory behind patchwork has always baffled me: why cut up all that fabric just to stitch it back together again? Here is my compromise: a plain little box with a cross-stitched patchwork lid.

Actual design measures:
4¼ in (10.5 cm) diameter

MATERIALS

1 piece of 14-count Aida in white measuring 8 in (20 cm) square
No. 22 tapestry needle
1 piece of card 4½ in (11.5 cm) diameter
Glue (rubber cement)
1 circular box 4½ in (11.5 cm) diameter

DMC Embroidery Cottons (floss):

1 skein of light pink (605)
1 skein of dark pink (603)
1 skein of perlé in light pink (605)

INSTRUCTIONS

Mark the centre of the chart and the centre of the fabric. Starting here, work in cross stitch using three strands of cotton (floss). When the design is complete, lightly press it on the wrong side over a soft towel.

Then lay the design face up on the backing card and trim leaving a 1 in (2.5 cm) selvedge. Fold the waste to the back of the card, and clip and glue to the back so that you have a neat finish. Carefully glue the mounted cross-stitch design to the box top.

Open out the skein of perlé and fold the thread into four. Make a twisted cord (see page 154) and glue it around the tucked edges of the box top. Trim off the ends, overlap them and glue them neatly into place.

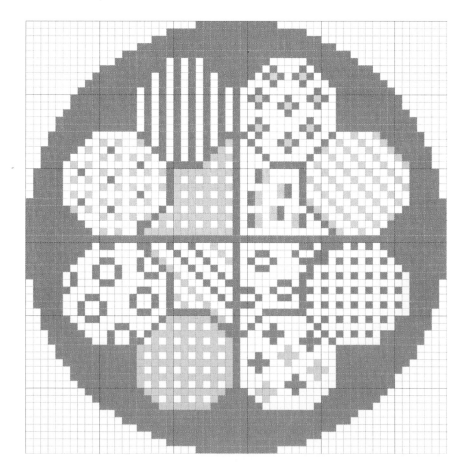

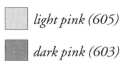 light pink (605)

dark pink (603)

PATCHWORK CLOCK

This patchwork design makes up into a pretty bedroom clock. Once you have stitched the hexagon shapes you could fill each block with designs of your choice. It is worked entirely in cross stitch with the exception of the clover stems, which are worked with one straight stitch.

Actual design measures:
8¼ × 8½ in (21 × 21.5 cm)

MATERIALS

1 piece of 14-count Aida in
white measuring 12 in
(30.5 cm) square
No. 22 tapestry needle
1 piece of backing card measuring
8¼ × 8½ in (21 × 21.5 cm)
Glue (rubber cement)
Knitting needle
Chapter ring or clock face measuring
3 in (7.5 cm) diameter
Clock works

DMC Embroidery
Cottons (floss):
1 skein of pale pink (3716)
1 skein of light yellow (744)
1 skein of green (564)
1 skein of lavender (340)
1 skein of blue (799)
1 skein of pink (962)
1 skein of green (913)
1 skein of yellow (743)

INSTRUCTIONS

Mark the centre of the chart and the centre of the fabric. Starting here, work in cross stitch using three strands of cotton (floss). When the design is complete, press it on the wrong side over a damp cloth, face down on a soft towel.

Then mount it on the backing card, gluing the waste edges to the back. Glue the clock face into position at the centre of the design. Find the very centre and gently push the knitting needle through the fabric and card, slitting the central threads of fabric as necessary. Insert the clock movement.

Top left of chart, continued on page 16

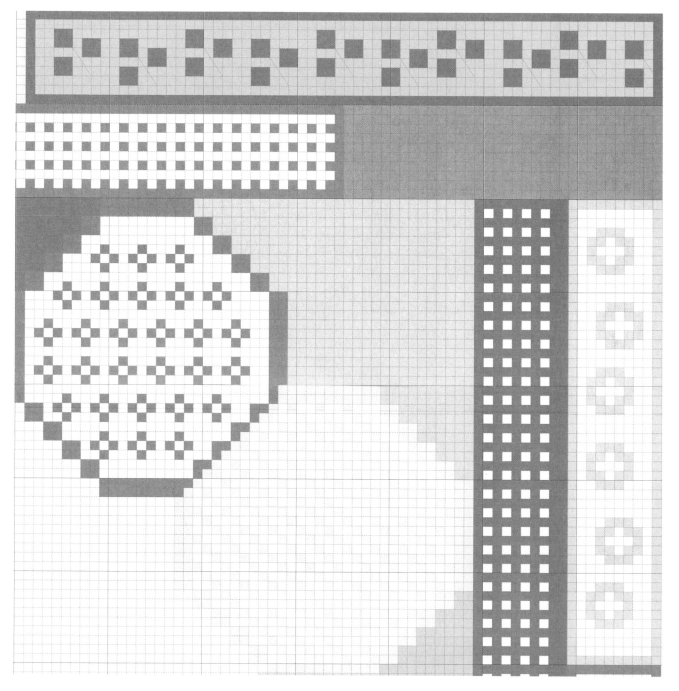

Top right of chart, continued on page 17

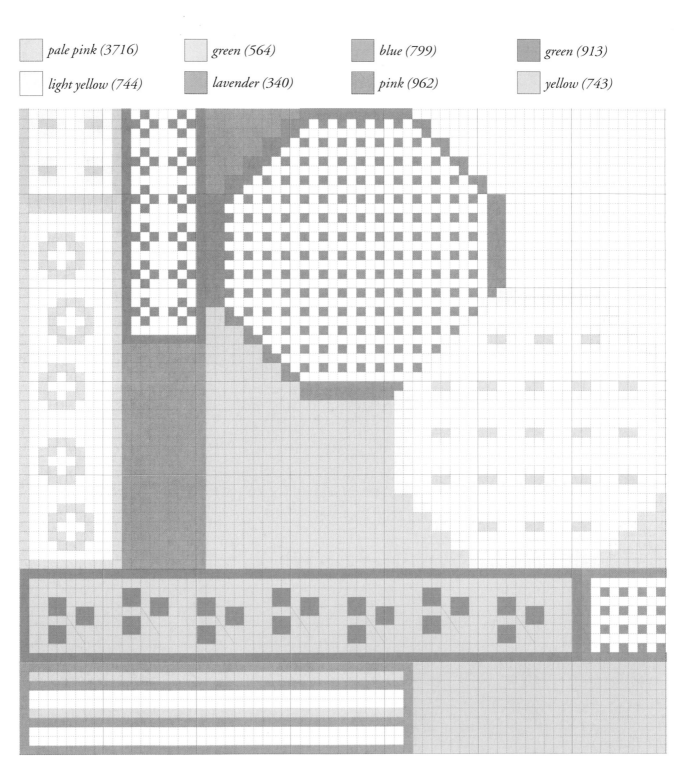

Bottom left of chart, continued from page 14

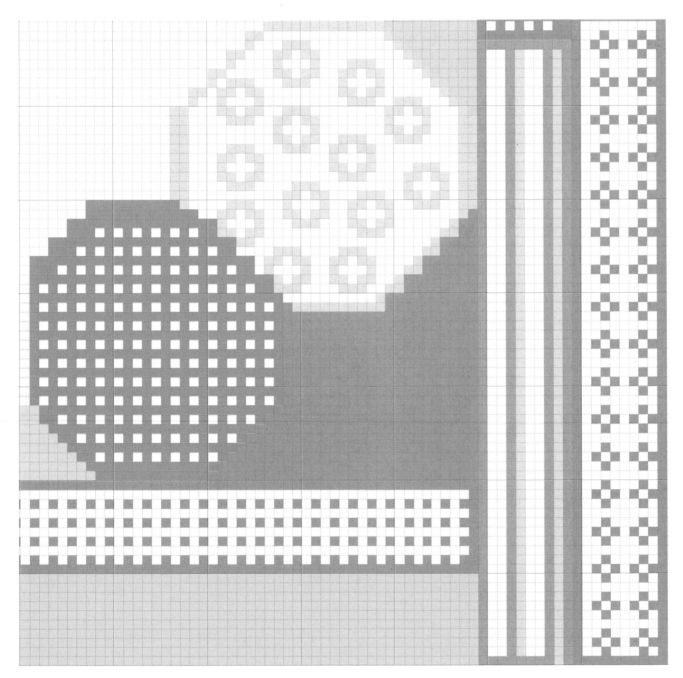

Bottom right of chart, continued from page 15

FRINGED
CHAMOIS BAG

This fringed bag can be worn attached to a belt and you can add as much or as little beading as you require. For added effect, you could stitch some more beads onto the fringing or even attach some feathers.

Actual design measures:
3¾ × 5¼ in (9.5 × 13.5 cm)

MATERIALS
1 piece of 28-count raw linen
  measuring 8 × 10 in
  (20 × 25.5 cm)
No. 26 tapestry needle
Seed beads in the following colours
  and quantities:
  maroon × 156
  blue × 156
  browny-green × 160
  yellow × 156
Sewing needle (or machine)
Cotton thread (to match the
  background fabric)
2 squares of chamois leather each
  measuring 12½ in
  (32 cm) square
Sharp scissors
Left-over waste lengths of chamois
  ½ in (1 cm) wide for plaiting

DMC Embroidery
Cottons (floss):
1 skein of blue (340)
1 skein of pink (603)
1 skein of red (321)
1 skein of yellow (3822)
1 skein of green (640)

INSTRUCTIONS
Mark the centre of the chart and the centre of the fabric. Starting here, work all the unbeaded cross-stitch areas over two threads of fabric using two strands of cotton (floss).

When these are complete, work the beaded areas using just one strand of cotton (floss). Work the first slant of your cross and on the return journey, slide a bead down the needle and, with it in position, complete the second half of the cross. When the design is complete, press it on the wrong side over a damp cloth, face down on a soft towel.

Then trim excess fabric leaving a ½ in (1 cm)-wide border. Trim the edges of the chamois leather just enough to create straight edges. Position your finished design on the centre of one piece of chamois and machine or hand stitch into place working flush to the edge stitches of your design. Fray the raw edges of the border fabric.

Make a ½ in (1 cm)-wide hem at the top edges of both pieces of chamois and machine or hand stitch down to form a neat edge. Now place the back and front pieces together, with the wrong sides facing.

Leaving 3 in (8 cm) of chamois free at the sides and bottom of the bag, machine or hand stitch the side and bottom seams. Next, carefully cut the waste chamois at the sides and bottom of the bag at ¼ in (5 mm) intervals to form a fringe.

To make the handle, cut waste chamois into ½ in (1 cm)-wide strips and make a three strip plait, joining in extra lengths as necessary until the plait is 37 ½ in (95 cm) long. Knot off the ends and stitch these to the top side edges of the bag.

blue (340)

pink (603)

red (321)

yellow (3822)

green (640) with brown beads

yellow (3822) with yellow beads

blue (340) with blue beads

red (321) with maroon beads

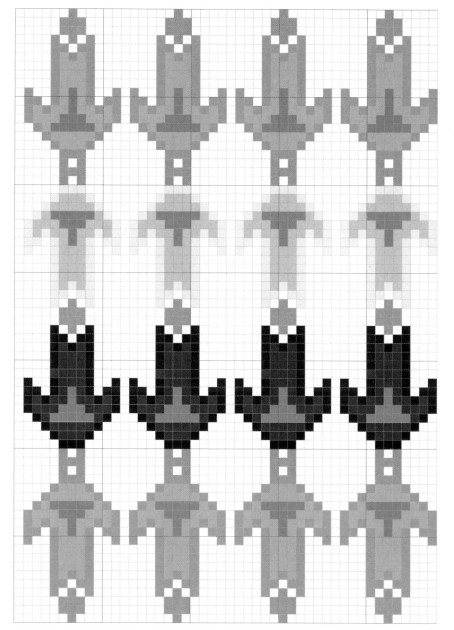

CHAMOIS WALLET

This pouch (see the photograph on page 19) can be used for credit cards, tobacco or even as a notebook cover. It is simply made and mounted on chamois leather. One large chamois leather (the type sold for cleaning windows) will make all the following beaded projects which are ideal as unusual gifts. The chamois is soft enough to stitch through with relative ease, but access to a sewing machine will assist you with the making-up process.

Actual design measures:
2¾ × 4¼ in (7 × 10.5 cm)

MATERIALS

1 piece of 28-count raw linen
    measuring 6 × 5 in (15 × 13 cm)
No. 26 tapestry needle
Seed beads in the following colours
    and quantities:
    red × 52
    blue × 36
    green × 100
    white × 42
Sewing needle
Cotton thread (to match the
    background fabric)
1 strip of chamois leather measuring
    17 × 6 in (43 × 15 cm)
Glue (rubber cement)

DMC Embroidery
Cottons (floss):
1 skein of red (606)
1 skein of blue (3746)
1 skein of green (906)
1 skein of yellow (741)
1 skein of white (blanc)
1 skein of black (310)

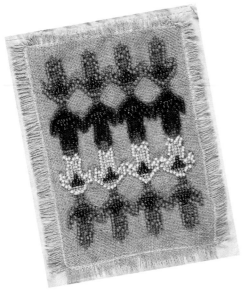

INSTRUCTIONS

Mark the centre of the chart and the centre of the fabric. Starting here, work all the unbeaded cross-stitch areas over two threads of fabric using two strands of cotton (floss).

When these are complete, work the beaded areas using just one strand of cotton (floss). Work the first slant of your cross and on the return journey, slide a bead down the needle and, with the bead in position, complete the second half of the cross. When the design is complete, press it on the wrong side over a damp cloth, face down on a soft towel.

Trim the edges of the chamois leather just enough to create straight edges. Fold the two short ends under so they leave a 1½ in (4 cm) gap in the middle. Fold in half again, aligning the previously folded edges. This forms a pouch with two pockets (you will glue this into position later). Trim around your design, leaving a ½ in (1 cm) border.

Now pin the panel to the centre front of your pouch. Open up the folds and stitch the panel as positioned through only one thickness of chamois. This can be done with a neat row of machine

stitches flush to the edges of the cross-stitch design or by hand. Once the design is secure, fray the raw edges of the border fabric.

Turn to the wrong side of the chamois and fold in the outer edges as before. Glue the side edges of the flaps into position.

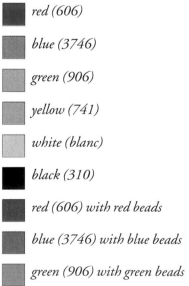

red (606)

blue (3746)

green (906)

yellow (741)

white (blanc)

black (310)

red (606) with red beads

blue (3746) with blue beads

green (906) with green beads

BEADED KEY FOB

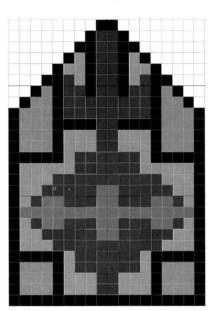

Here is an idea for using up any scraps of chamois you have left over from larger projects. In addition to the key fob, you could also use the same principle to make earrings, a bracelet, a pendant or a brooch.

Actual design measures:
1½ × 2 in (4 × 5 cm)

MATERIALS
1 piece of 28-count raw linen
measuring 4 × 5 in (10 × 13 cm)
No. 26 tapestry needle
Seed beads in the following colours
and quantities:
red × 84
green × 36
Sewing needle (or machine)
Cotton thread (to match the
background fabric)
1 piece of chamois leather measuring
3¼ in (8 cm) square
Sharp scissors
Key ring attachment

DMC Embroidery
Cottons (floss):
1 skein of red (606)
1 skein of yellow (741)
1 skein of blue (3746)
1 skein of green (906)
1 skein of black (310)

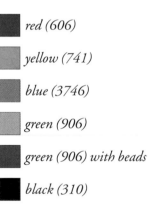

red (606)

yellow (741)

blue (3746)

green (906)

green (906) with beads

black (310)

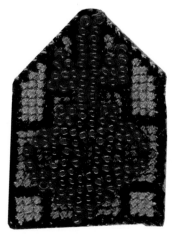

INSTRUCTIONS
Mark the centre of the chart and the centre of the fabric. Starting here, work all the unbeaded cross-stitch areas over two threads of fabric using two strands of cotton (floss).

When these are complete, work the beaded areas using just one strand of cotton (floss). Work the first slant of your cross and on the return journey, slide a bead down the needle and, with it in position, complete the second half of the cross. When the design is complete, press it on the wrong side over a damp cloth, face down on a soft towel.

Then trim any excess fabric to leave a ½ in (1 cm)-wide border. Fold in the edges of the fabric to the edge of the design and stick onto the chamois leather so that the central point of the embroidery is in the centre of one side of the chamois square.

Trim the chamois to match the photograph on page 19 and fringe along the sides and bottom. Tuck the end of the key ring into the top of the fob and stitch firmly in place.

INSPIRATION
FROM EUROPE

When it comes to style and elegance, Europeans have always had the edge. Whether your taste is for floral flamboyance or stark simplicity, I hope you find something here to please you. To get in the mood I have used an abundance of gold thread and rich fabrics, but you should choose your colours to coordinate with your room style. France features heavily in this section. The fleur-de-lis shape has always conjured up a wealth of design ideas. If you choose to make the cushion or box top (see pages 32-7 and 49-51), try stencilling a fleur-de-lis onto wooden or fabric accessories to make the overall image complete.

MC
ABCD EFGHI
IKLMNOPQRSTUV
WXYZ abcdefghijklmnopq
rstuvwxyz
1234567890

TRADITIONAL SAMPLER

This sampler was produced in Germany in the 1800s by Magdalena Friedrichson. Instead of a message or proverb, I have included a chart for the alphabet. In the spirit of the original piece you might like to use the letters to make your own statement on the embroidery instead.

Actual design measures:
18 × 16¾ in (45.5 × 42.5 cm)

Frame measures:
21½ × 20½ in (54.5 × 52 cm)

MATERIALS
1 piece of 28-count Cashel linen in
ecru measuring 23½ × 22½ in
(60 × 57 cm)
No. 24 tapestry needle

DMC Embroidery
Cottons (floss):
1 skeins of greeny grey (372)
3 skeins of rusty red (900)
1 skein of turquoise (807)
1 skein of lilac (316)
1 skein of gold (977)
1 skein of green (522)
2 skeins of chestnut (919)
1 skein of white (blanc)
1 skein of petrol (3765)
2 skeins of black (310)

INSTRUCTIONS
Mark the centre of the chart and the centre of the fabric. Starting here, work in cross stitch over two strands of fabric using two strands of cotton (floss). When the design is complete, press it on the wrong side over a damp cloth, face down on a soft towel. Mount the design on a board and frame as you wish.

Top left of chart, continued on page 30

greeny grey (372)		turquoise (807)		gold (977)		chestnut (919)		petrol (3765)
rusty red (900)		lilac (316)		green (522)		white (blanc)		black (310)

Top right of chart continued on page 31

Bottom left of chart, continued from page 28

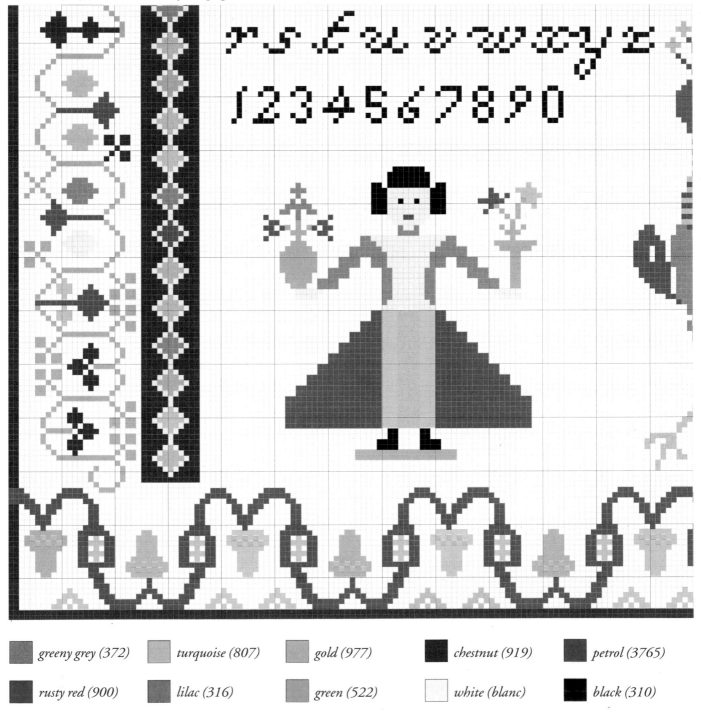

	greeny grey (372)		turquoise (807)		gold (977)		chestnut (919)		petrol (3765)
	rusty red (900)		lilac (316)		green (522)		white (blanc)		black (310)

Bottom right of chart, continued from page 29

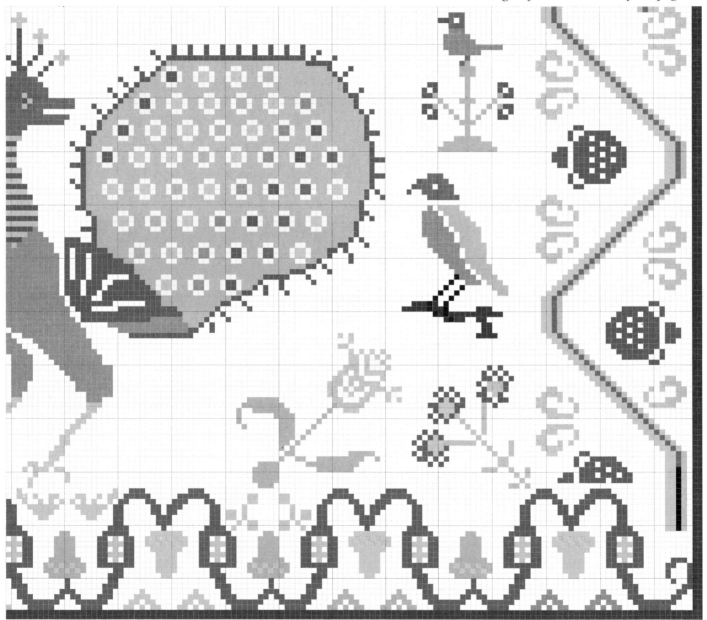

FLEUR-DE-LIS CUSHION

This cushion is worked on a textured silk and backed with blue velvet. Unless you are an experienced cross stitcher I would suggest using a smooth silk fabric because otherwise you might find it difficult to keep your stitch tension even. If you select a fine silk, back the finished design with an iron-on interfacing before making up the cushion.

Actual design measures:
13 in (33 cm) square

MATERIALS

1 piece of pure silk fabric in beige measuring 17 in (43 cm) square
1 piece of 14-count waste canvas measuring 16 in (40.5 cm) square
No. 8 crewel needle
Tweezers
1 piece of iron-on interfacing measuring 13 in (34 cm) square (optional)
2 pieces of velvet backing fabric measuring 10 × 14½ in (25.5 × 36 cm)
1 strip of same measuring 59 × 1½ in (150 × 4 cm)
1 length of piping cord measuring 59 in (150 cm)
Cotton thread (to match the background fabric)

DMC Embroidery Cottons (floss):

1 skein of red (3801)
1 skein of dark blue (792)
1 skein of fuchsia (3804)
1 skein of pink (3806)
1 skein of ginger (722)
1 skein of gold (742)
1 skein of butter(744)
1 skein of green (906)
1 skein of lime (907)
2 skeins of cream (746)
1 skein of coffee (3828)

DMC Metallic Thread:
1 reel of light gold (282)

INSTRUCTIONS

Tack (baste) the waste fabric to the centre of the silk. Mark the centre of the chart and the centre of the waste fabric. Starting here, work in cross stitch using two strands of cotton (floss). Use gold thread straight from the reel.

When the design is complete, carefully remove the tacking (basting) and pull the threads of waste canvas from under the embroidery with tweezers. Now work the flower stems in coffee and lime backstitch. Then press the design on the wrong side over a damp cloth, face down on a soft towel. Back the completed design with iron-on interfacing if required. Trim the fabric to allow ⅝ in (1.5 cm) seam allowance around the design.

On both pieces of backing fabric make a 1 in (2.5 cm)-wide hem across one long end. These now form two halves of the cushion back.

To make the piping, lay the piping cord at the centre of the wrong side of the long strip of fabric and fold the fabric in half, wrong sides together. Stitch through both thicknesses of the fabric flush to, and enclosing, the cord. Pin the piping around the edge of the embroidery, matching the trimmed seams and clipping into the corners. Then, with right sides together, pin one half of the backing fabric into place, with the seamed edge in the centre. Stitch into position along the outside edges.

Do the same with the second half of backing, allowing it to overlap the first half at the centre. Trim the seams and turn right sides out. Insert a cushion pad through the opening.

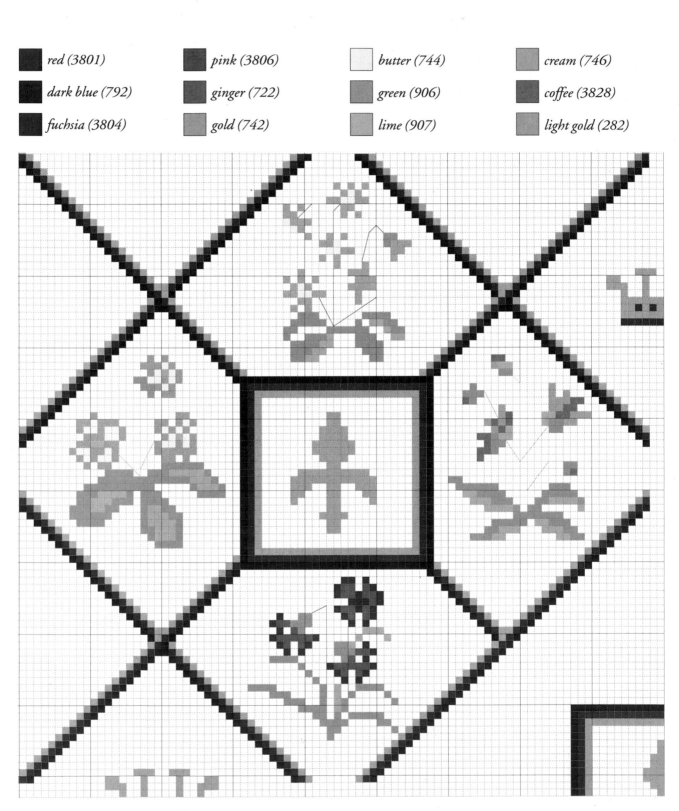

	red (3801)		pink (3806)		butter (744)		cream (746)
	dark blue (792)		ginger (722)		green (906)		coffee (3828)
	fuchsia (3804)		gold (742)		lime (907)		light gold (282)

Top left of chart, continued on page 36

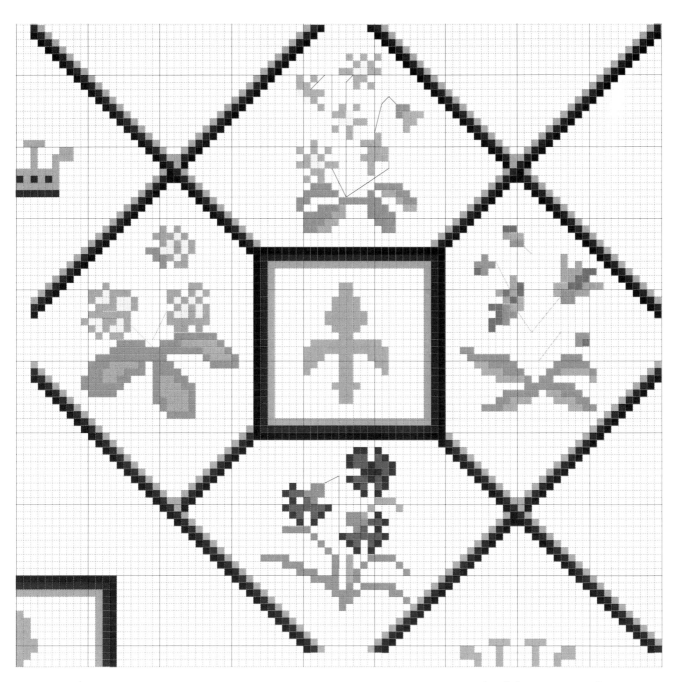

Top right of chart, continued on page 37

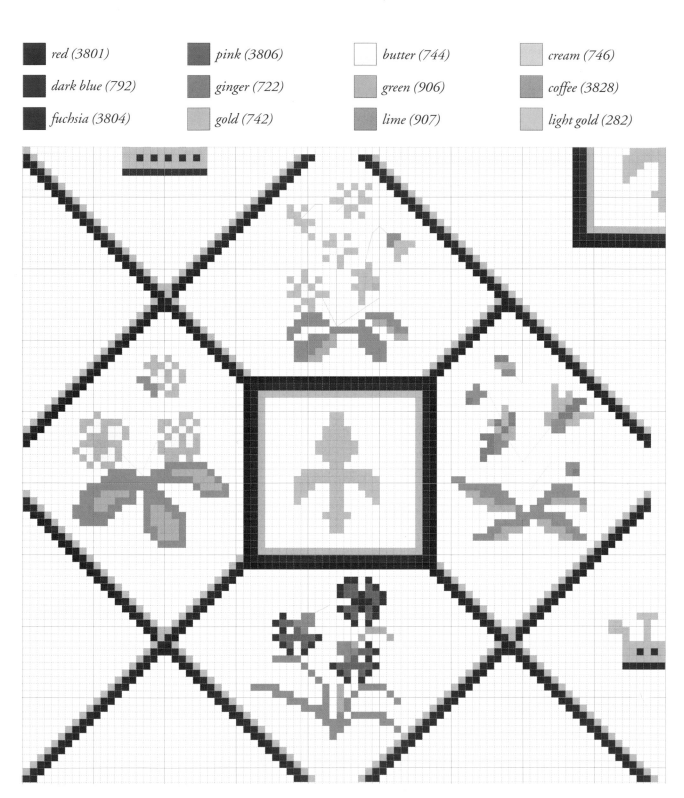

red (3801)   pink (3806)   butter (744)   cream (746)

dark blue (792)   ginger (722)   green (906)   coffee (3828)

fuchsia (3804)   gold (742)   lime (907)   light gold (282)

Bottom left of chart, continued from page 34

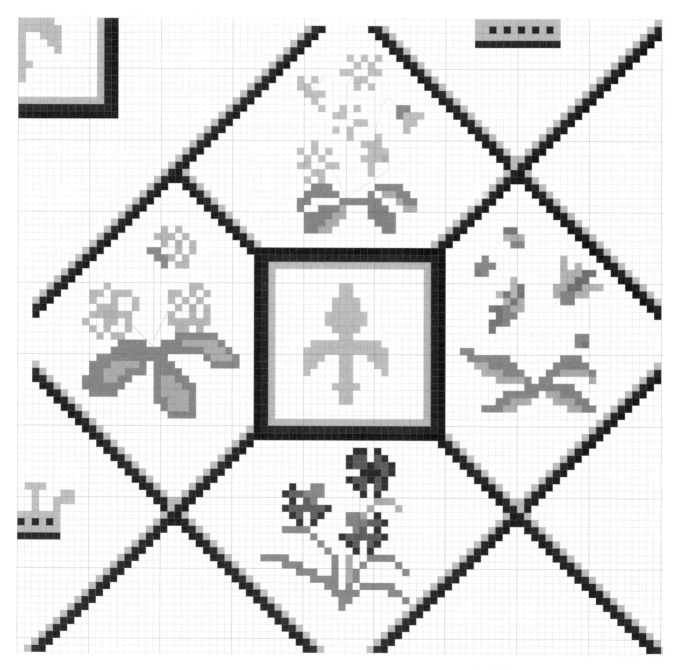

Bottom right of chart, continued from page 35

ROSE TABLECLOTH

This design was inspired by a design on an early 18th-century Frenchman's waistcoat and I hope you will agree that it translates well onto this tablecloth. Cheap imported cutwork cloths are widely available in the stores.

Centre design measures:
5 × 6½ in (13 × 16.5 cm)

Single motifs measure:
1¾ × 1¼ in (4.5 × 3 cm)

MATERIALS

White tablecloth measuring 34 in (86.5 cm) square
1 piece of 14-count waste canvas measuring 7 × 8 in (18 × 20 cm)
16 pieces of same measuring 2½ in (6.5 cm) square
No. 8 crewel needle
Tweezers
Cotton thread

DMC Embroidery Cottons (floss):

1 skein of mid-rose (961)
1 skein of rose (962)
1 skein of pink (3716)
1 skein of red (606)
1 skein of crimson (600)
1 skein of purple (208)
1 skein of lilac (210)
1 skein of gold (726)
1 skein of lemon (727)
1 skein of dark green (580)
1 skein of green (581)
1 skein of ecru (712)

INSTRUCTIONS

Take the large piece of waste canvas and tack (baste) it onto the centre of the tablecloth. Now arrange the small pieces randomly over the cloth following the photograph on page 42.

Mark the centre of each chart below and opposite and the centre of each piece of waste canvas. Starting each motif here, work in cross stitch using two strands of cotton (floss). When the cross stitch is complete, carefully remove the tacking (basting) and then pull out the strands of waste canvas from under the stitches using the tweezers. Press the tablecloth on the wrong side over a damp cloth, face down on a soft towel.

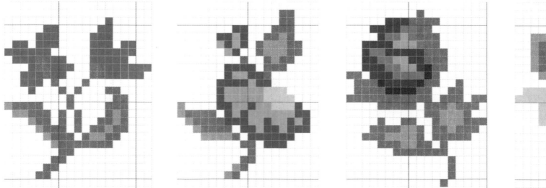

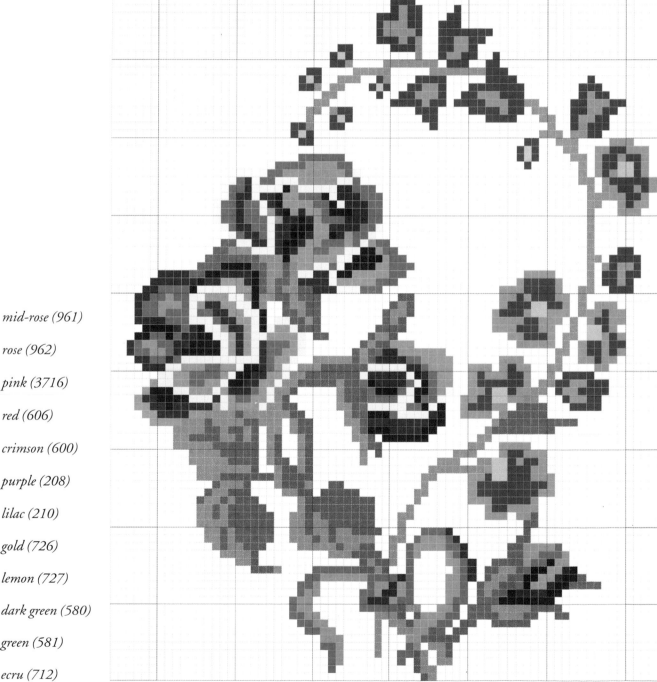

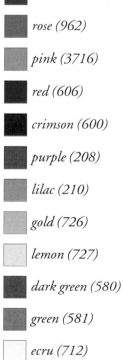

mid-rose (961)

rose (962)

pink (3716)

red (606)

crimson (600)

purple (208)

lilac (210)

gold (726)

lemon (727)

dark green (580)

green (581)

ecru (712)

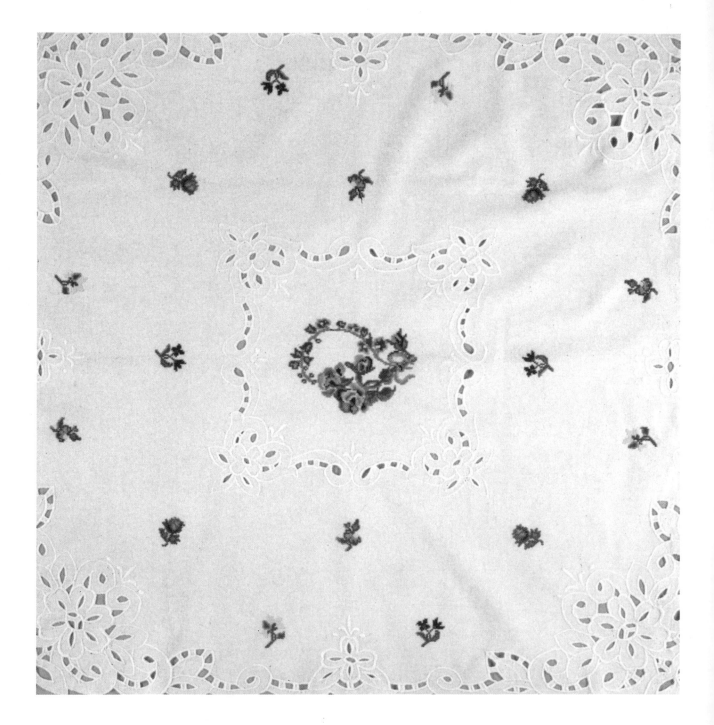

SILK POCHETTE

This sister project to the Silk Cushion featured on pages 46-8 is made up into a pochette in which you can keep your precious jewellery. Add a gilt chain and it will serve as a very pretty evening bag.

Actual design measures: 5½ in (14 cm) square

MATERIALS

1 piece of medium-weight blue silk measuring 20 × 10 in (51 × 25.5 cm)
1 piece of 14-count waste canvas measuring 7 in (18 cm) square
No. 8 crewel needle
Tweezers
1 piece of lining measuring 20 × 10 in (51 × 25.5 cm)
1 length of gold piping cord measuring 35 in (89 cm)
Cotton threads (to match the fabric)
Sewing needle
1 piece of ¹/₁₀ in (2 mm)-wide ribbon measuring 8 in (20 cm)
2 gold buttons

DMC Metallic Thread:

1 reel of light gold (282)

INSTRUCTIONS

On the piece of blue silk, position the square of waste canvas centrally widthwise, leaving 4½ in (11.5 cm) of blue silk free at the top (short) end. Mark the centre of the chart and the centre of the waste canvas. Starting here, work in cross stitch using the thread straight from the reel. When the cross stitch is complete, carefully remove the tacking (basting) and then pull out the strands of waste canvas from under the stitches using the tweezers. Press the silk on the wrong side over a damp cloth, face down on a soft towel.

Place the worked blue silk on the lining fabric with right sides facing and make a seam around three of the outer edges. Leave the short edge at the top open and also 2 in (5 cm) at the top of each side seam. Turn the right way out. Take the bottom edge of the bag and fold it up to form an envelope, still leaving the 2 in (5 cm) of both silk and lining free at the top edge to form a fold-over flap.

Fold in the raw edges of fabric on the flap inserting the gold piping cord between the blue silk and the lining. Also insert the piping between the front and back of the main body of the bag. Tack (baste) the piping in place and then stitch up the sides of the bag and the sides and top of the flap. Place the bag face down and sew on the two gold buttons, positioning them 2 in (5 cm) in from the edges.

Cut the ribbon in half and fold one piece in half again to form a small loop. Stitch this to the edge of the bag flap to correspond with the button. Repeat for the second button loop.

SILK CUSHION

This classical Greek design has been worked in gold thread on a background of richly coloured silk. The tile shape could also be worked on Aida fabric and mounted to form a coaster.

Actual design measures:
5½ in (14 cm) square

MATERIALS

1 piece of medium-weight blue silk measuring 7 in (18 cm) square
1 piece of 14-count waste canvas measuring 7 in (18 cm) square
No. 8 crewel needle
Tweezers
1 piece of red silk measuring 12 in (30.5 cm) square
1 piece of same measuring 12 × 10 in (30.5 × 25.5 cm)
1 piece of same measuring 12 × 4 in (30.5 × 10 cm)
Sewing needle (or machine)
Cotton threads (to match the fabrics)
1 length of gold piping cord measuring 47 in (120 cm)
Wadding (synthetic batting) to pad cushion

DMC Metallic Thread:
1 reel of light gold (282)

INSTRUCTIONS

Take the square of waste canvas and tack (baste) it onto the centre of the blue silk. Mark the centre of the chart and the centre of the waste canvas. Starting here, work in cross stitch using the thread straight from the reel. When the cross stitch is complete, carefully remove the tacking (basting) and then pull out the strands of waste canvas from under the stitches using the tweezers. Press the silk on the wrong side over a damp cloth, face down on a soft towel.

Centre the work on the right side of the square of red silk. Turn in the raw edges of the embroidered panel, pin into place and then stitch this on with a row of back stitches all around the outer edge of the blue fabric.

Make a ½ in (1 cm)-wide hem around the edges of the red fabric (use a machine if preferred). Now pin the gold piping cord into position around the edge, on the wrong side of the fabric. Take the two remaining pieces of red fabric and make a ½ in (1 cm)-wide hem around these, too.

Lay the pieces on the back of the

cushion front with wrong sides facing so that the narrow strip slightly overlaps the wider strip and the piping is sandwiched neatly between the back and front pieces. Pin, tack (baste) and stitch these pieces together around the outer edge. Insert the wadding (batting) through the back opening.

FLEUR-DE-LIS BOX TOP

Cheap imported baskets and boxes are easily obtainable and make a good foil for your cross stitch. Here, I have taken part of the pattern for the Fleur-de-lis Cushion (see pages 32-7) and made it up into a panel. The size of panel depends on the size of your box or basket, so buy that first!

Actual design measures:
6½ in (16 cm) square

MATERIALS
1 piece of 14-count Aida fabric in blue measuring 8 in (20 cm) square (or 2 in [5 cm] larger than your box top)
No. 22 tapestry needle
1 piece of wadding (synthetic batting) measuring same size as box top
1 piece of card measuring same size as box top
Glue (rubber cement)

DMC Embroidery Cottons (floss):
1 skein of red (3801)
1 skein of dark blue (792)
1 skein of fuchsia (3804)
1 skein of pink (3806)
1 skein of ginger (722)
1 skein of gold (742)
1 skein of butter (744)
1 skein of green (906)
1 skein of lime (907)
2 skeins of cream (746)
1 skein of coffee (3828)

DMC Metallic Thread:
1 reel of light gold (282)

INSTRUCTIONS
Mark the centre of the chart and the centre of the fabric. Starting here, work in cross stitch using three strands of cotton (floss). Use the gold thread straight from the reel. Work the flower stems in coffee and lime backstitch. When the design is complete, press it on the wrong side over a damp cloth, face down on a soft towel.

Glue the wadding (batting) onto the card and leave to dry. Stretch the cross-stitched piece over the wadding (batting) being careful to centre the design. Glue the raw edges of fabric to the back of the card. Glue the mounted work to the box top.

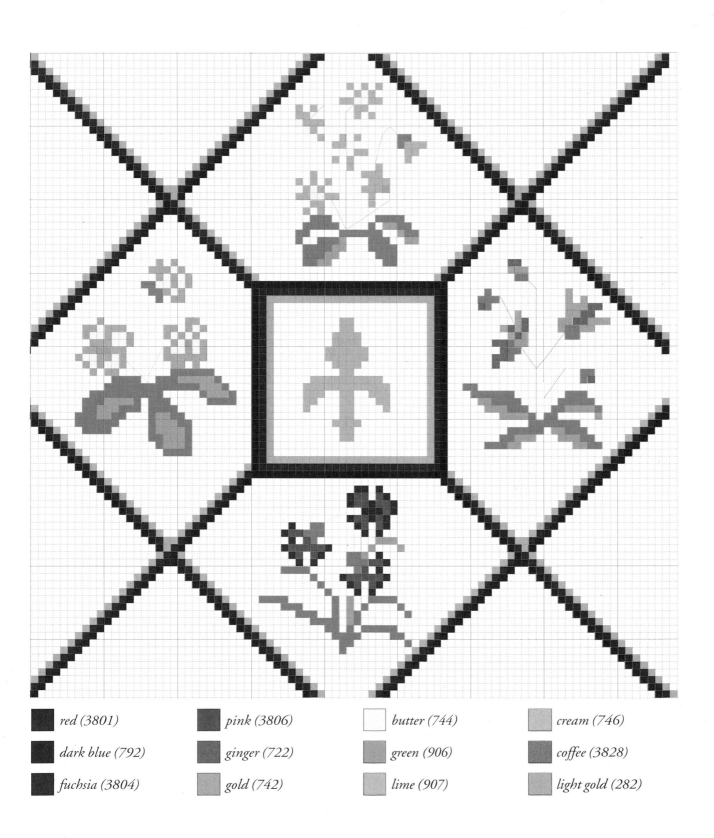

	red (3801)		pink (3806)		butter (744)		cream (746)
	dark blue (792)		ginger (722)		green (906)		coffee (3828)
	fuchsia (3804)		gold (742)		lime (907)		light gold (282)

THE ART OF
THE CELTS

The term Celt relates to a number of tribes who never established a single nation. During the pagan and Christian eras they travelled extensively from their origins in Eastern Europe reaching Britain and Europe in around 250BC. Their art uses geometry to illustrate an inner world and they are fantastically precise. Extraordinary images were recorded in *The Book of Kells*, an illuminated manuscript housed at Trinity College in Dublin. In this section I have used basic knotwork designs, which translate particularly well into cross stitch, to create a choice of project ideas.

PICTURE FRAME

It seemed appropriate to produce a Celtic design on pure linen, and this frame could be used for a picture or a mirror. I incorporated gold thread to emulate the richness of an illuminated manuscript, the earthy colours would sit well against plain brickwork or on a shelf filled with terracotta pots.

Actual design measures:
8¾ × 10¾ in (22 × 27 cm)

MATERIALS
1 piece of 28-count raw linen
measuring 12½ × 15 in
(32 × 38 cm)
No. 24 tapestry needle
2 pieces of backing card measuring
8¾ × 10¾ in (22 × 27 cm)
Craft knife
1 piece of wadding (synthetic
batting) measuring
8¾ × 10¾ in (22 × 27 cm)
Glue (rubber cement)
Self-adhesive picture hook

DMC Embroidery Cottons (floss):
1 skein of blue (340)
1 skein of green (563)
3 skeins of chestnut (919)

DMC Metallic Thread:
3 reels of light gold (282)

INSTRUCTIONS
Mark the centre of the chart and the centre of the fabric. Starting here, work in cross stitch over two threads of fabric using three strands of cotton (floss). Use the gold thread straight from the reel. When the design is complete, press it on the wrong side over a damp cloth, face down on a soft towel.

Take one of the pieces of card and, with the craft knife, cut a 6 × 4 in (15 × 10 cm) oblong from the centre. Do the same with the wadding (synthetic batting) and then glue it onto the front of the frame. Stretch your finished cross-stitched piece over the padded frame and glue the raw outside edges to the back.

Make cuts from the centre of the fabric to each inside corner of the frame. Fold the fabric to the back of the card, then stretch, trim the excess, and glue into place. On the remaining piece of card, dab glue around the bottom edge and along the sides. Glue this to the back of your design. Leave to dry. Slide your photograph in through the top and finally attach a self-adhesive hook to the back.

Top left of chart, continued on page 58

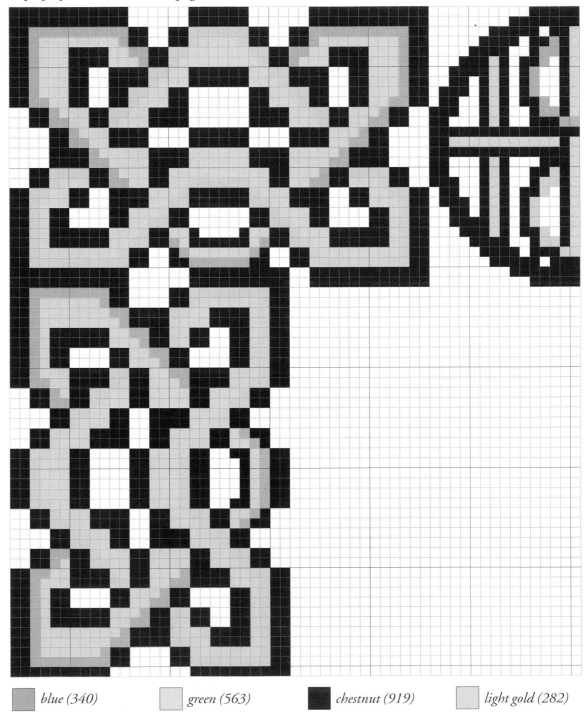

 blue (340)   green (563)   chestnut (919)   light gold (282)

Top right of chart, continued on page 59

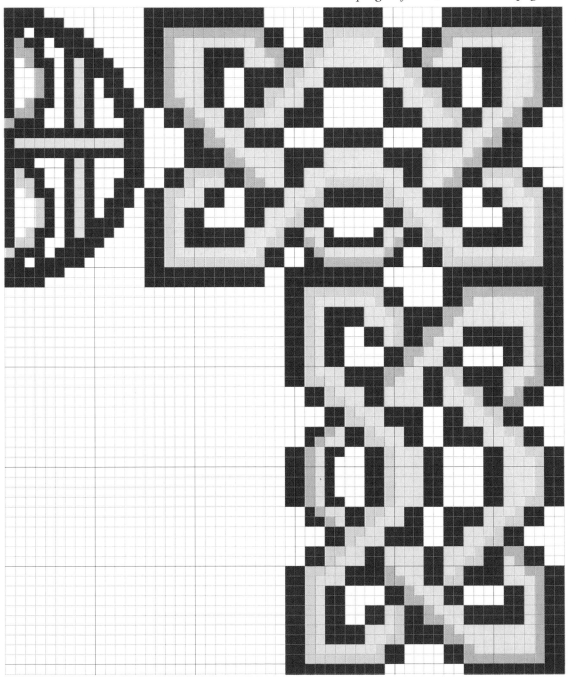

Bottom left of chart, continued from page 56

| | blue (340) | | green (563) | | chestnut (919) | | light gold (282) |

Bottom right of chart, continued from page 57

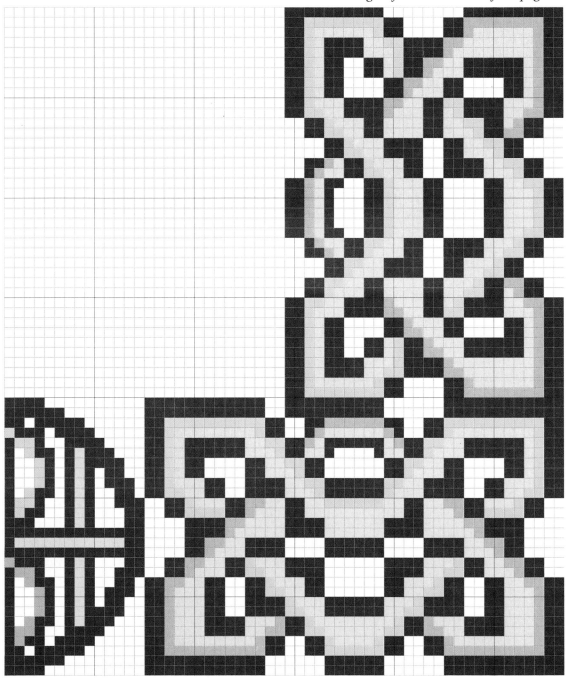

KNOTWORK BOX TOP

I have used this panel to form a box top. The design could also be used for a book cover (see pages 63-5). The pattern is taken from traditional knotwork although there is nothing traditional about the colours I have selected. When choosing colours, don't forget to consider the fabric colour as part of your design.

Actual design measures:
7¾ × 5½ in (19.5 × 14 cm)

MATERIALS

1 piece of 16-count Aida in light khaki measuring 12 × 9½ in (30.5 × 24 cm)
No. 24 tapestry needle
1 piece of wadding (synthetic batting) measuring 7¾ × 5½ in (19.5 × 14 cm)
Glue (rubber cement)
1 piece of card measuring 7¾ × 5½ in (19.5 × 14 cm)
Wooden box

DMC Embroidery Cottons (floss):

1 skein of red (326)
1 skein of mauve (552)

INSTRUCTIONS

Mark the centre of the chart and the centre of the fabric. Starting here, work in cross stitch using two strands of cotton (floss). When the design is complete, press it on the wrong side over a damp cloth, face down on a soft towel.

Glue the wadding (batting) to the front of the piece of card and leave to dry. Then stretch the cross-stitched piece over the covered card, centring the design carefully and glue the raw edges to the back. Glue the covered panel to the top of the box.

red (326)

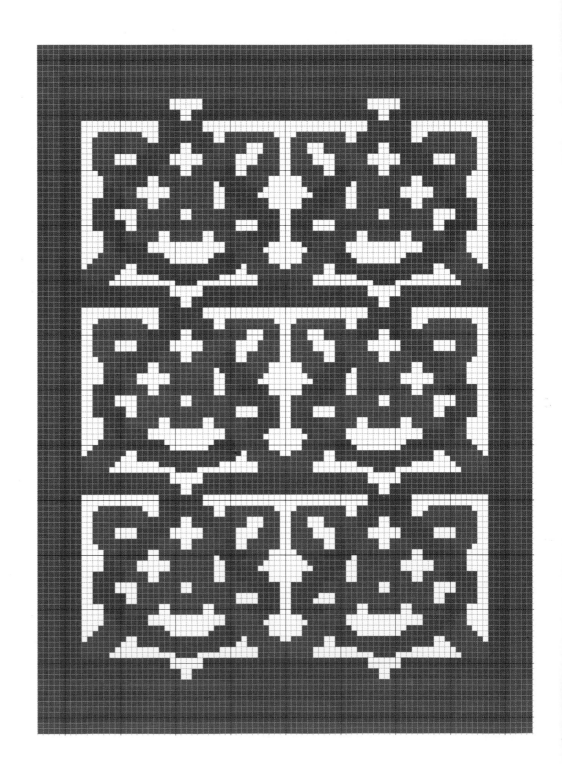 mauve (552)

STITCHED BOOK COVER

Covering a book with fabric is extremely easy and very rewarding. Embroiderers have been doing it for centuries, starting with early Bibles richly embellished with goldwork, and progressing to address books neatly dressed in art nouveau prints. Here I have used Aida because it is a substantial fabric that will result in clean folded edges.

Actual design measures:
5¼ × 7½ in (13.5 × 19 cm)

MATERIALS
1 piece of 14-count Aida in red
measuring 16 × 12 in
(40.5 × 30.5 cm)
No. 22 tapestry needle
1 book measuring 6 × 8½ in
(15 × 21.5 cm)
Glue (rubber cement)
1 A4 sheet of white or coloured
lightweight card

DMC Embroidery Cottons (floss):
1 skein of gold (734)
1 skein of purple (552)
1 skein of green (991)

DMC Metallic Thread:
1 reel of light gold (282)

INSTRUCTIONS
Fold the fabric in half horizontally, so that the fold is on your left. Mark the centre of the chart and the centre of the front piece of fabric. Starting here, work in cross stitch using three strands of cotton (floss). When the design is complete, press it on the wrong side over a damp cloth, face down on a soft towel.

Lie the fabric face down on a table, place the book on top so that the spine sits in the fold. Dab glue on the inside front edges of the back and front book covers, stretch the fabric over the book, turn the edges over the covers and press down on the glued areas.

Slit the fabric on either side of the spine at the top and bottom. Dab with glue and tuck the ends into the book spine. Fold in the top and bottom edges and glue into position, taking care to keep the corners neat.

Using leftover lengths of thread, make a twisted cord (see page 154) that is 16½ in (42 cm) long (we have used two lengths of purple [552], two of green [991] and eight of gold [734]). Tie off the bottom of the cord and open up the threads to form a tassel. Dab glue on the top of the cord and tuck it into the book spine.

Finally, cut an oblong of card to fit the inside of the front cover and glue it over the rough edges of fabric. Repeat for back cover.

gold (734)

purple (552)

green (991)

light gold (282)

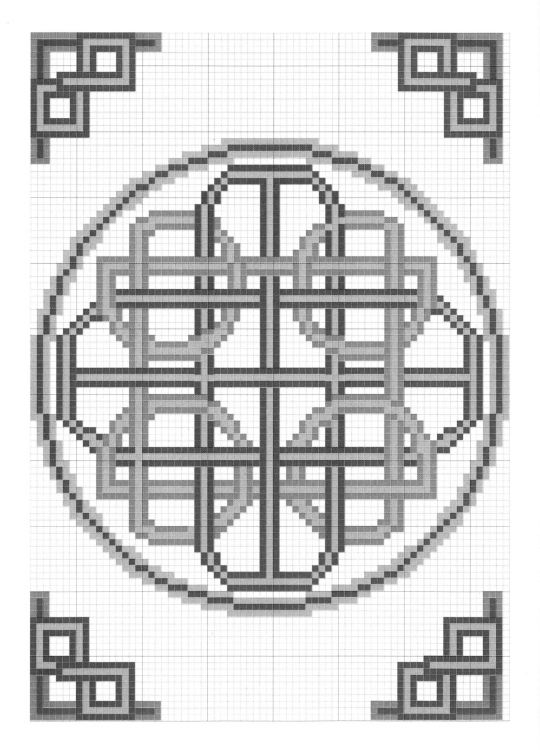

PATTERNED PINCUSHION

An illusion of complex knots can be created by repeating and mirroring simple knots. A rich texture is added to the design by covering all of the fabric with cross stitch. Simple to create, this is one of my favourite projects.

Actual design measures:
3 in (7.5 cm) square

MATERIALS
1 piece of 18-count Aida measuring
5 in (13 cm) square
No. 25 tapestry needle
1 piece of backing fabric measuring
5 in (13 cm) square
Cotton thread (to match the
background fabric)
Small amount of wadding
(synthetic batting)

1 length of gold cord or trim
for edging measuring
12½ in (32 cm)

DMC Embroidery
Cottons (floss):
1 skein of red (321)
1 skein of green (702)
1 skein of purple (550)

DMC Metallic Thread:
1 reel of light gold (282)

INSTRUCTIONS
Mark the centre of the chart and the centre of the fabric. Starting here, work in cross stitch using two strands of cotton (floss). Use the gold thread straight from the reel. When the design is complete, press it on the wrong side over a damp cloth, face down on a soft towel.

Place the design on the backing fabric, right sides facing, and stitch up three seams, flush to the design. Trim excess fabric, turn right way out and insert wadding (batting). Tuck in waste fabric on the open edge and top sew the seam leaving a small ¼ in (5 mm) opening.

Tuck one end of the cord into the opening and catch it around the sides with the light gold thread. Tuck the remaining end of the cord into the opening and stitch shut.

■ red (321)

■ green (702)

■ purple (550)

□ light gold (282)

CELTIC BIRD
HANGING

This Celtic bird was taken from *The Book of Kells*. He is very famous and is often depicted in Celtic design. The hanging rods are available in various lengths from Framecraft (see Stockists on page 156) and provide you with an instant way to display your cross stitch.

Actual design measures:
3¾ × 10½ in (9.5 × 26.5 cm)

MATERIALS
1 piece of 14-count Aida in ecru measuring 8 × 14 in (20 × 35.5 cm)
No. 22 tapestry needle
1 piece of backing fabric measuring 6 × 14½ in (15 × 37 cm)
7 in (18 cm)-long hanger
Cotton thread (to match the backing fabric)
Sewing needle

DMC Embroidery Cottons (floss):
2 skeins of blue (826)
2 skeins of wine (3803)
2 skeins of gold (3820)
2 skeins of green (989)
1 skein of black (310)

INSTRUCTIONS
Mark the centre of the chart and the centre of the fabric. Starting here, work in cross stitch using three strands of cotton (floss). When the design is complete, press it on the wrong side over a damp cloth, face down on a soft towel.

Place the design on the backing fabric with right sides facing and seam around the side and bottom edges. Turn it the right way out, tuck in the excess fabric along the open seam and top sew to close.

With a length of six-strand wine cotton (floss) (3803), join the top of the design to the hanger rod, looping the thread over the bar and through the Aida, figure-of-eight fashion. Make four tassels (see page 155), each using ten 8 in (20 cm) lengths of wine cotton (floss) and, spacing them evenly, stitch these to the bottom of the hanging.

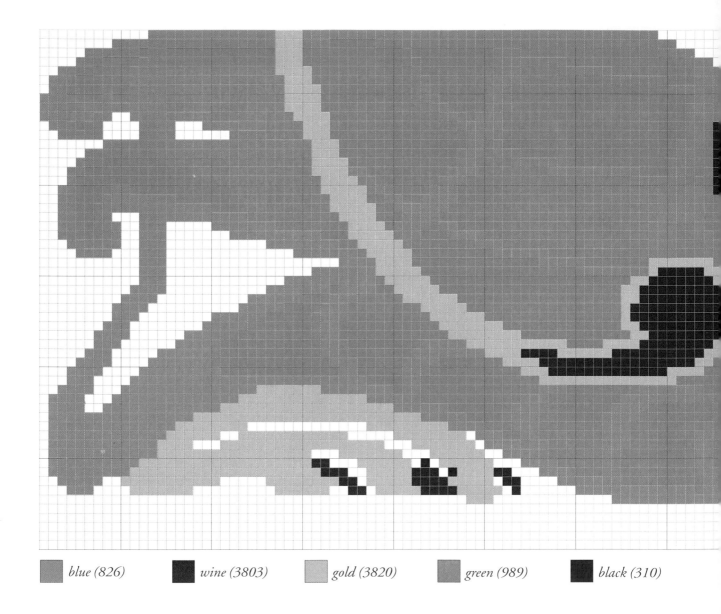

blue (826)   wine (3803)   gold (3820)   green (989)   black (310)

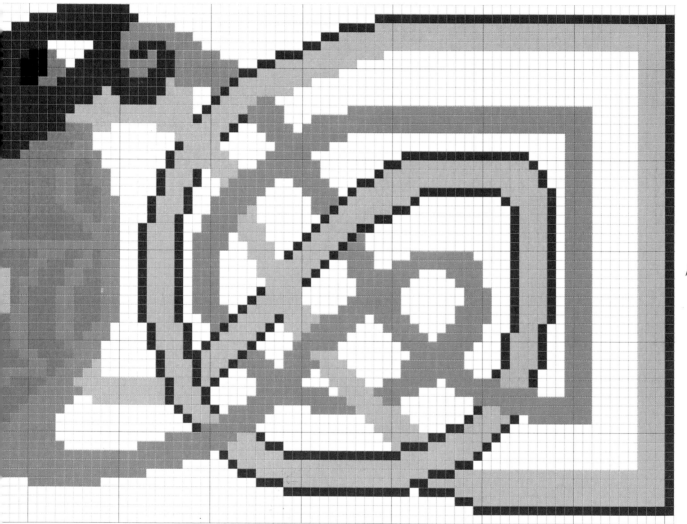

Top of hanging

SCANDINAVIAN STYLE

Scandinavians love their cross stitch and, traditionally, many homes display different cross-stitched furnishings and table linens designed to welcome each new season. The images I have chosen for this section are taken from historic samplers and textiles and are used in a contemporary way. Some of the motifs are quite famous and may be familiar to you. As with many cultures the themes of Scandinavian design have their roots in paganism, but the links between the Scandinavian countries are strengthened by a shared mythology that makes them quite unique.

LACE-TRIMMED TABLECLOTH

This pretty tablecloth owes its motifs to a Norwegian sampler produced in 1818. I like the crisp contrasts of the red, white and blue, but you could, of course, change the colour scheme to match your furnishings. The cloth itself, complete with lace trim in place, is available by mail order (see Stockists on page 156).

The motifs are designed to fit in an area 4 in (10 cm) square

MATERIALS
Lace tablecloth measuring 34 in (86 cm) square with defined squared-off areas
16 pieces of 14-count waste canvas each measuring 4 in (10 cm) square
No. 8 crewel needle
Cotton thread
Tweezers

DMC Embroidery Cottons (floss):
2 skeins of red (349)
1 skein of blue (798)

INSTRUCTIONS
Tack (baste) each square of waste canvas over a square defined on the tablecloth. Mark the centre of each chart and the centre of each piece of waste canvas. Starting each motif here, work in cross stitch using two strands of cotton (floss), positioning the motifs according to the plan to the left.

When the design is complete, carefully remove the tacking (basting) threads and then pull out the strands of waste canvas from under the stitches using the tweezers. Press the tablecloth on the wrong side over a damp cloth, face down on a soft towel. Note that the finished designs lie at an angle.

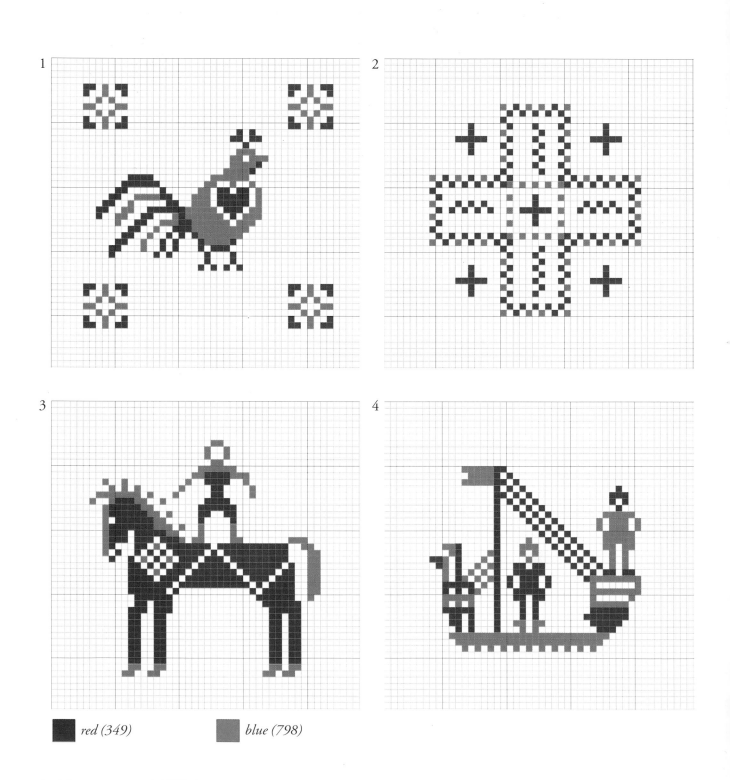

red (349)   blue (798)

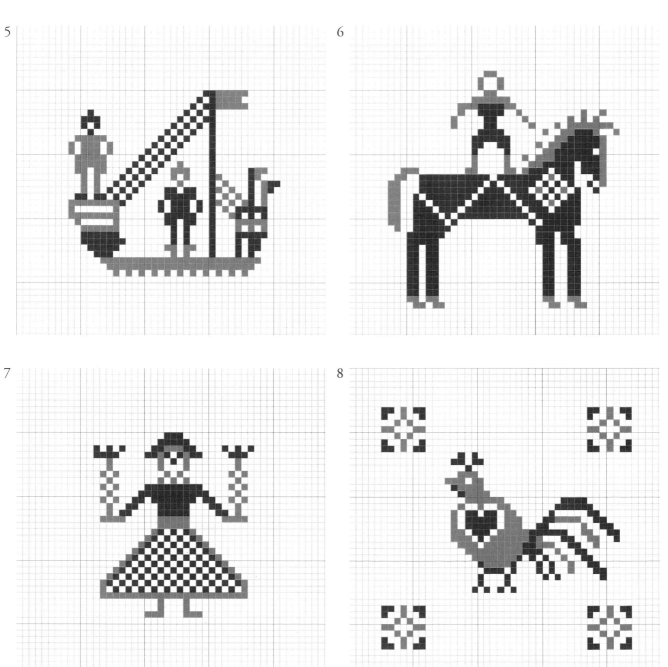

5

6

7

8

SNOWFLAKE SAMPLER BAG

These jolly women, standing in a garden full of snowflakes and peacocks, are backed with gingham and serve as a tote bag. Purists might like to frame them and hang them on a wall instead.

Actual design measures:
9 × 13½ in (23 × 34 cm)

MATERIALS
1 piece of 14-count Aida in red
   measuring 13 × 18 in
   (33 × 45.5 cm)
1 piece of gingham cotton fabric
   measuring 13 × 18 in
   (33 × 45.5 cm)
No. 22 tapestry needle
Cotton thread (to match the Aida)
1 length of white cord measuring
   45 in (114 cm)
2 wooden beads

DMC Embroidery Cottons (floss):
4 skeins of ecru (746)

INSTRUCTIONS
Mark the centre of the chart and the centre of the Aida. Starting here, work in cross stitch using two strands of cotton (floss). When the design is complete, press it on the wrong side over a damp cloth, face down on a soft towel.

Lay the design over the gingham fabric with right sides facing. Stitch around the side and bottom edges to form a bag, and hem the top seam. Turn the bag right side out and attach the cord to the top corners, threading it through the beads for decoration.

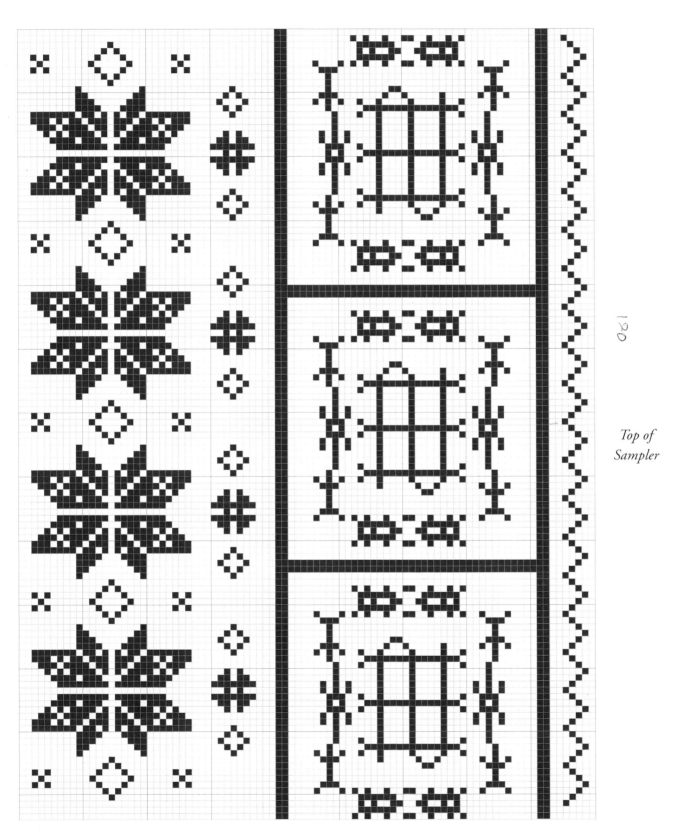

*Top of
Sampler*

CURTAIN TIEBACK

Here I have used the women from the Snowflake Sampler Bag design featured on pages 78-81 to make a curtain tie. If you don't like to involve yourself in making up projects, look in your needlework store for Aida and linen ready-made bands. Repeat the design until you fill the length of band you require and then tie it in a bow around your curtain.

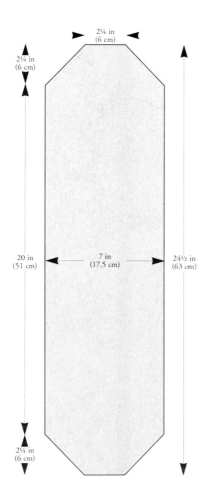

Actual design measures:
17 × 4¼ in (43 × 10.5 cm)

MATERIALS
1 piece of 14-count Aida in white measuring 20 × 8 in (51 × 20 cm)
No. 24 tapestry needle
1 piece of stiff interfacing measuring 18 × 5 in (45.5 × 13 cm)
1 piece of red backing fabric measuring 25 × 8 in (63.5 × 20 cm)
Cotton threads (red and white)
Sewing needle (or machine)
Two 3 in (7.5 cm)-diameter curtain rings

DMC Embroidery Cotton (floss):
3 skeins of red (349)

INSTRUCTIONS
Mark the centre of the chart and the centre of the Aida. Starting here, work in cross stitch using three strands of cotton (floss). When the design is complete, press it on the wrong side over a damp cloth, face down on a soft towel.

Place the strip of interfacing at the centre back of the design and lay both the design and interfacing face up on the centre of the strip of backing fabric. Turn under the raw edges of Aida and machine or hand stitch into place on the backing. Referring to the diagram on the left, cut off the sides and corners of the backing fabric and make a ¼ in (5 mm)-wide double hem all around the edges. Sew the rings into position at the centre of each end.

BALDISHOL WARRIOR

This famous warrior was created in the 12th century and re-discovered in the 19th century in a church at Baldishol in Norway. Forming part of the larger Baldishol tapestry in which each section depicts different months of the year, he represents the month of May. He is a companion project to the Dove Key Panel (see pages 87-9) which appeared in the same tapestry denoting April.

Actual design measures:
8 × 9 in (20 × 23 cm)

MATERIALS

1 piece of 14-count Rustico Aida measuring 12 × 13 in (30.5 × 33 cm) or 4 in (10 cm) larger than your mounting board
No. 24 tapestry needle
1 piece of mounting board to fit your cupboard front

DMC Embroidery Cottons (floss):

2 skeins of black (310)
2 skeins of dark grey (317)
1 skein of mid-grey (451)
1 skein of stone (642)
2 skeins of barley (437)
1 skein of butter (677)
1 skein of coffee (3045)
2 skeins of red (606)
1 skein of ecru (746)
1 skein of light grey (318)

INSTRUCTIONS

Mark the centre of the chart and the centre of the fabric. Starting here, work the main part of the design in cross stitch using two strands of cotton (floss) throughout and filling in the detail lines on the armour in ecru backstitch. When the design is complete, press it on the wrong side over a damp cloth, face down on a soft towel.

Centre the design on the card and glue the raw edges of the fabric to the back. Note that we have sized the canvas to fit a custom-made cupboard (see Stockists on page 156), but the panel can be sized to fit the front of any recess. Alternatively, it could be framed or used as a box top or a photo album cover.

DOVE KEY PANEL

These doves, extracted from the Baldishol tapestry (see page 84), represent April and would make a good birthday gift for anyone born in that month. Here they are mounted to form a panel suitable for keys.

Actual design measures:
13 × 5¼ in (33 × 13.5 cm)

MATERIALS
*1 piece of 14-count Aida in red
   measuring 17 × 9½ in
   (43 × 24 cm)*
No. 24 tapestry needle

*1 piece of mounting board
   measuring 13½ × 5¾ in
   (34 × 14.5 cm)*
Glue (rubber cement)
*1 piece of plywood or hardboard
   measuring 17½ × 9¾ in
   (44 × 24.5 cm)*

2 lengths of 2 in (5 cm) battening each measuring 13½ in (34 cm)
2 lengths of 2 in (5 cm) battening each measuring 9¾ in (24.5 cm)
Wood glue or panel pins
Screw-in hooks for keys

DMC Embroidery Cottons (floss):
1 skein of dark grey (317)
1 skein of stone (642)
2 skeins of barley (437)
2 skeins of butter (677)
1 skein of ecru (746)
2 skeins of black (310)

INSTRUCTIONS

Mark the centre of the chart and the centre of the fabric. Starting here, work in cross stitch using three strands of cotton (floss). When the design is complete, press it on the wrong side over a damp cloth, face down on a soft towel.

Stretch the fabric over the mounting board (see page 154)

and glue the raw edges to the back.

Lay the battening on the plywood to form a frame. Either glue the strips into position with wood glue and leave to dry, or nail them into place through the back of the wood.

Glue the cross-stitched panel to the centre of the framed board.

dark grey (317)

stone (642)

barley (437)

butter (677)

ecru (746)

black (310)

RUSSIAN, HUNGARIAN AND POLISH DESIGNS

Eastern Europe provides a real wealth of inspiration for designers. Much of the embroidery originates with the decoration of peasant costume but many of the motifs have travelled extensively and can be found in a number of cultures. Here, a design from Poland sits next to a Russian geometric motif and the Turkish-influenced floral designs of Hungary. I have turned to museum pieces as my resource for this section, using motifs and panels from much larger compositions and translating them from freestyle embroidery to cross stitch.

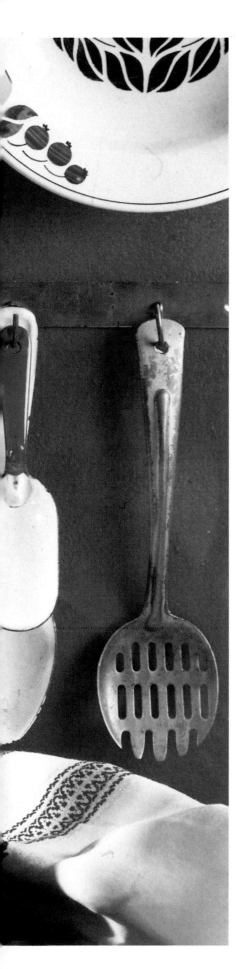

FLORAL SALT BOX

This bright little design began its life decorating a bridegroom's costume in Mezokovesd, Hungary. Here it is put to more practical use as the front panel of a salt box.

Actual design measures:
3¼ × 2½ in
(8 × 6.5 cm)

MATERIALS
1 piece of 14-count Aida in black
measuring 7 × 6½ in
(18 × 16.5 cm)
No. 22 tapestry needle
1 piece of card measuring
4 × 3 in (10 × 7.5 cm)
Glue (rubber cement)
Wooden salt box

DMC Embroidery
Cottons (floss):
1 skein of fuchsia (602)
1 skein of pink (604)
1 skein of pale green (472)
1 skein of green (703)
1 skein of ginger (977)
1 skein of blue (792)
1 skein of yellow (725)
1 skein of white (blanc)
1 skein of red (606)

INSTRUCTIONS
Mark the centre of the chart and the centre of the fabric. Starting here, work in cross stitch using three strands of cotton (floss). When the design is complete, press it on the wrong side over a damp cloth, face down on a soft towel.

Stretch the design over the card and, taking care to centre the design, glue the raw edges to the back. Glue the finished panel to the front of the salt box.

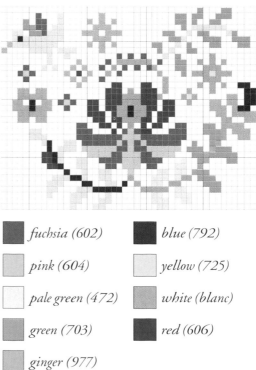

■ fuchsia (602)		■ blue (792)	
pink (604)		yellow (725)	
pale green (472)		white (blanc)	
green (703)		■ red (606)	
ginger (977)			

PERCHING BIRDS WALLHANGING

These bright and beautiful birds originally decorated a bedspread embroidered at the end of the 1800s in Alfold, Hungary. Here, they are worked entirely in cross stitch and mounted on red felt to make a wallhanging.

Actual design measures:
4½ × 15½ in (11.5 × 39 cm)

MATERIALS
1 piece of 18-count Aida in ice blue measuring 17½ × 8 in (44 × 20 cm)
No. 25 tapestry needle
1 piece of felt measuring 22 × 8 in (56 × 20 cm)
12 in (30.5 cm) wooden hanging rod
Cotton thread (to match the Aida)
Sewing needle (or machine)

DMC Embroidery Cottons (floss):
1 skein of fuchsia (602)
1 skein of pale green (472)
1 skein of green (703)
1 skein of dark green (701)
1 skein of ginger (977)
1 skein of blue (792)
1 skein of yellow (725)
1 skein of red (606)

INSTRUCTIONS
Mark the centre of the chart and the centre of the fabric. Starting here, work in cross stitch using two strands of cotton (floss). When the design is complete, press it on the wrong side over a damp cloth, face down on a soft towel.

Make a 2½ in (6.5 cm)-wide hem at the top (short end) of the felt to hold the hanger. Position the design at the centre of the felt and turn in the edges leaving a 1 in (2.5 cm) border on each side of the design. Stitch the panel onto the felt by machine or with a row of back stitches around the outer edge. Thread the hanger through the top hem.

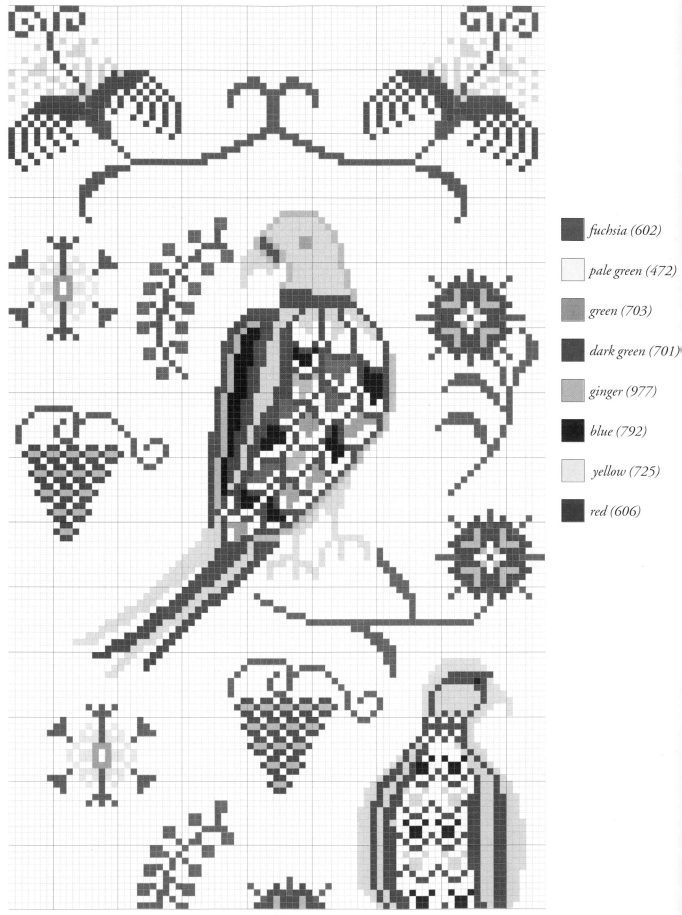

fuchsia (602)

pale green (472)

green (703)

dark green (701)

ginger (977)

blue (792)

yellow (725)

red (606)

Join to top of chart opposite

STAR KEY CUPBOARD

This geometric Russian design began life as part of a lady's costume, tied like a back-to-front apron around her waist. Here it is used as a panel on a key cupboard, but it would make an equally smart box top or even a place mat.

Actual design measures:
4 × 7¼ in (10 × 18.5 cm)

MATERIALS
1 piece of 14-count Aida in red
   measuring 8 × 11 in
   (20 × 28 cm)
No. 22 tapestry needle
1 piece of card measuring 4 × 7¼ in
   (10 × 18.5 cm)
Glue (rubber cement)
Wooden key cupboard

DMC Embroidery Cottons (floss):
1 skein of blue (796)
1 skein of gold (742)
1 skein of white (blanc)

INSTRUCTIONS
Mark the centre of the chart and the centre of the fabric. Starting here, work in cross stitch using two strands of cotton (floss). When the design is complete, press it on the wrong side over a damp cloth, face down on a soft towel.

Stretch the design over the card and, taking care to centre the design, glue the raw edges to the back. Glue the finished panel to the front of the key cupboard.

blue (796)

gold (742)

white (blanc)

LACE-EDGED NAPKIN

This floral motif was designed for the corner of a head scarf and is used here as the corner of a square, lace-edged napkin. I have used 14-count waste canvas but you could use 11-count to make the design bigger and stitch it onto a matching tablecloth.

Actual design measures:
6 in (15 cm) square

MATERIALS
Lace-trimmed serviette (ours measures 15 in [38 cm] square)
1 piece of 14-count waste canvas measuring 7 in (18 cm) square
Cotton thread
No. 8 crewel needle
Tweezers

DMC Embroidery Cotton (floss):
1 skein of black (310)

INSTRUCTIONS
Pin the canvas into position at the corner of the serviette and tack (baste) into place. Mark the centre of the chart and the centre of the waste canvas. Starting here, work in cross stitch using two strands of cotton (floss).

When the cross stitch is complete, carefully remove the tacking (basting) thread and then pull out the strands of waste canvas from under the stitches with tweezers. Work the stems in backstitch. Press the stitching on the wrong side over a damp cloth, face down on a soft towel.

IMAGES FROM AUSTRALASIA

Australia is a wonderful mix of native tradition and original thinking. The selection of designs that follow are all inspired by Aboriginal art which translates wonderfully into contemporary designs. I have also included a chart of Billy Bluegum, my very first teddy/koala who accompanied me on a childhood trip down under. Space restricted me from including the amazing flowers and bird life that are an intrinsic part of the Australian lifestyle, but try using your own favourite images in some of the project ideas.

BILLY BLUEGUM

Here is my best friend, sitting, as he does, in a gum tree. He is worked on Jobelan fabric but he would be just as happy on Aida if that is the fabric you prefer to use. With a simple backing, he makes up into a friendly bag, suitable for a child.

Actual design measures:
5½ × 5¼ in (14 × 13.5 cm)

MATERIALS

1 piece of Jobelan 28-count fabric
*   in pale mauve measuring*
*   12 × 10½ in (30.5 × 26.5 cm)*
1 piece of backing fabric measuring
*   7 × 16 in (18 × 40.5 cm)*
No. 24 tapestry needle
Sewing needle
Cotton thread (to match
*   the backing)*
1 length of cord measuring
*   32 in (82 cm)*

DMC Embroidery
Cottons (floss):
1 skein of green (580)
1 skein of brown (400)
1 skein of dark grey (413)
1 skein of mid-grey (646)
1 skein of light grey (648)
1 skein of white (blanc)
1 skein of black (310)

INSTRUCTIONS

Mark the centre of the chart and the centre of the fabric. Starting here, work in cross stitch over two threads of fabric using two strands of cotton (floss). When the design is complete, press it on the wrong side over a damp cloth, face down on a soft towel.

Fold the backing fabric in half (with the fold at the bottom) with wrong sides facing, and centre the design on the front half. Stitch the design to the fabric along the bottom edge. Fold in and stitch down a 2 in (5 cm) hem at both top edges of fabric. Turn to the wrong side and sew up the two side seams through both the design and backing fabric. Turn to right side and attach the cord for the handle, stitching this to each top corner.

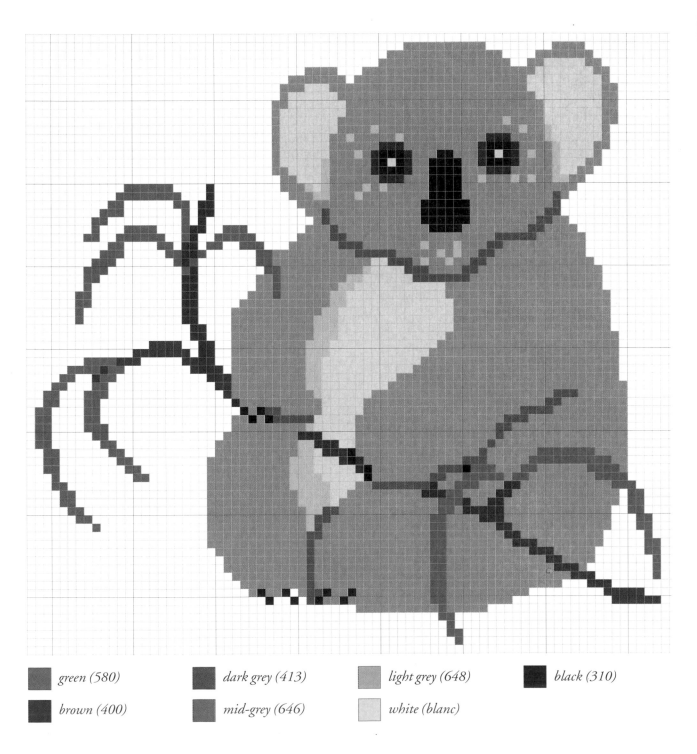

SNAPPY CROC

This young fellow is more dangerous than he looks. Inspired by a Wandjina cave painting, he should only take a few hours to stitch and will find a good home on your bathroom wall.

Actual design measures:
3 × 5½ in (7.5 × 14 cm)

MATERIALS

1 piece of Jobelan 28-count fabric in dark rose measuring 7 × 9½ in (18 × 24 cm)
No. 24 tapestry needle
Picture frame measuring 4 × 6 in (10 × 15 cm)

DMC Embroidery Cottons (floss):

1 skein of black (310)
1 skein of gold (3820)
1 skein of white (blanc)

INSTRUCTIONS

Mark the centre of the chart and the centre of the fabric. Starting here, work in cross stitch over two threads of fabric using three strands of cotton (floss). Add the backstitch detail in black. When the design is complete, press it on the wrong side over a soft towel and mount it in the frame.

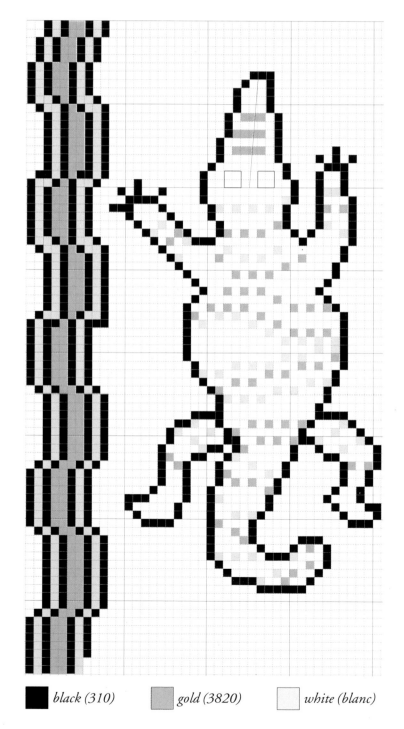

■ black (310)　　▨ gold (3820)　　□ white (blanc)

FISHY TALE

This fish was originally found swimming over a bark painting that illustrated the saga of the *Opossum Tree*, one of the oldest legends of Arnhem Land. He was designed by me as a companion to the crocodile featured on page 107 and should follow him wherever he goes.

Actual design measures:
3 × 3¼ in (7.5 × 8 cm)

MATERIALS
1 piece of Jobelan 28-count fabric in dark rose measuring 7 × 7½ in (18 × 19 cm)
No. 24 tapestry needle
Picture frame measuring 3½ in (9 cm) square

DMC Embroidery Cottons (floss):
1 skein of black (310)
1 skein of gold (3820)
1 skein of white (blanc)

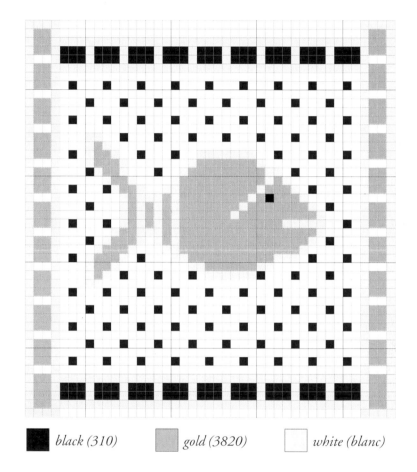

■ *black (310)*   ■ *gold (3820)*   □ *white (blanc)*

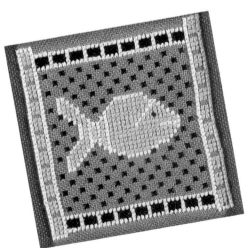

INSTRUCTIONS
Mark the centre of the chart and the centre of the fabric. Starting here, work in cross stitch over two threads of fabric using three strands of cotton (floss). Add a black French knot for the eye. When the design is complete, press it on the wrong side over a soft towel and mount it in the frame.

Two Jabirus and a Spoonbill

These three characters come from the mythical island of Bralku where all human spirits go after death. They are illustrated on an Arnhem Land bark painting where they herald the arrival of another spirit. You can put them on your fridge or wear them as brooches or necklaces. They are friendly folk so take care of them.

Actual design measures:
Standing aborigine
2¼ × 3½ in (5.5 × 9 cm)
Stooping aborigine
2¾ × 2¼ in (7 × 5.5 cm)
Spoonbill
2¼ × 2½ in (5.5 × 6.5 cm)

MATERIALS
1 piece of 14-count paper canvas in manila measuring 6 × 8 in (15 × 20 cm)
Sharp paper scissors
No. 24 tapestry needle
1 piece of backing card measuring 6 × 8 in (15 × 20 cm)
Glue (rubber cement)
Brooch back, small magnet or leather thong as desired

DMC Embroidery Cottons (floss):
1 skein of terracotta (3830)
1 skein of black (310)
1 skein of white (blanc)

INSTRUCTIONS
Cut the paper canvas into three pieces matching the sizes of the designs plus a surround of four holes of blank canvas. Mark the centre of each chart and the centre of each piece of canvas. Starting here, work each design in cross stitch using three strands of cotton (floss). Work white French knots for the eyes. When the designs are complete trim away any excess canvas with a pair of sharp scissors and press on the wrong side over a damp cloth, face down on a soft towel.

Cut a piece of backing card to the size of each design and glue to the back. Stick a brooch mount or magnet to the centre back of the card or, to make a necklace, make two holes through the top of the card and canvas, insert a leather thong and knot each end to secure.

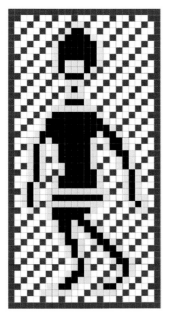

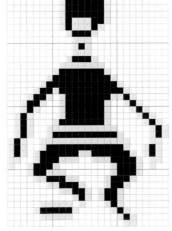

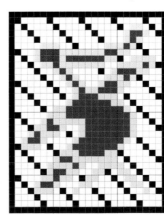

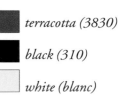

terracotta (3830)

black (310)

white (blanc)

TREASURES FROM AFAR

Some of my favourite embroidered designs began life in India and Afghanistan, although these do not immediately suggest the use of cross stitch. The daily work of women is embodied in the bold, bright images that adorn clothing and domestic textiles, and I wonder at the combination of simple motifs and intricate stitching that went into their creation. In this section I have used familiar motifs in unfamiliar circumstances and added some shells and buttons for good measure. I was pleased at how easily the motifs seemed to translate into cross stitch and I hope you enjoy the results.

BIRD MIRROR

This project is easy to produce on Aida and will make a bright addition to a contemporary interior. The bird motif is interchangeable with the elephant and the lion who appear later in this section on pages 120-3. You could even add some beads or shisha mirrors to the corner sections to make it extra special.

Actual design measures:
11½ in (29 cm) square

MATERIALS

1 piece of 14-count Aida in black measuring 13½ in (34 cm) square
No. 22 tapestry needle
40 small pearl buttons (with four holes for stitching on)
2 pieces of card each measuring 11½ in (29 cm) square
Craft knife
1 piece of wadding (synthetic batting) measuring 11½ in (29 cm) square
Glue (rubber cement)
1 mirror tile measuring 6 in (15 cm) square
Self-adhesive picture hook or card for strut

Anchor Marlitt Threads:

3 skeins of pink (814)
4 skeins of red (1017)
3 skeins of blue (817)
3 skeins of mauve (816)
1 skein of yellow (822)
3 skeins of green (1030)
1 skein of grey (846)
2 skeins of kingfisher (1055)

INSTRUCTIONS

Leaving a 2 in (5 cm)-wide border of fabric all around the design, begin by working the outline. Work in cross stitch using two strands of Marlitt, completing all the normal sized cross stitches first and then stitching the large crosses over three blocks of fabric (there will be two empty holes under each cross section of thread). Then stitch the buttons into position working a cross in the centre of each to secure. When the design is complete, press it on the wrong side over a damp cloth, face down on a soft towel.

Take one of the pieces of card and, with the craft knife, cut a 5½ in (14 cm) square from the centre. Do the same with the wadding (batting) and then glue it onto the front of the frame.

Stretch your finished cross-stitched piece over the padded frame and glue the raw outside edges to the back. Make cuts from the centre of the fabric to each inside corner of the frame. Fold the fabric to the back of the card, then stretch, trim off the excess and glue into place.

Glue the mirror firmly to the centre of the remaining piece of card, leave to dry and then glue the frame on top of the mirror and backing card. Attach the self-adhesive hook to the back of the backing card or use sticky tape to position a supporting cardboard strut.

Top left of chart, continued on page 118

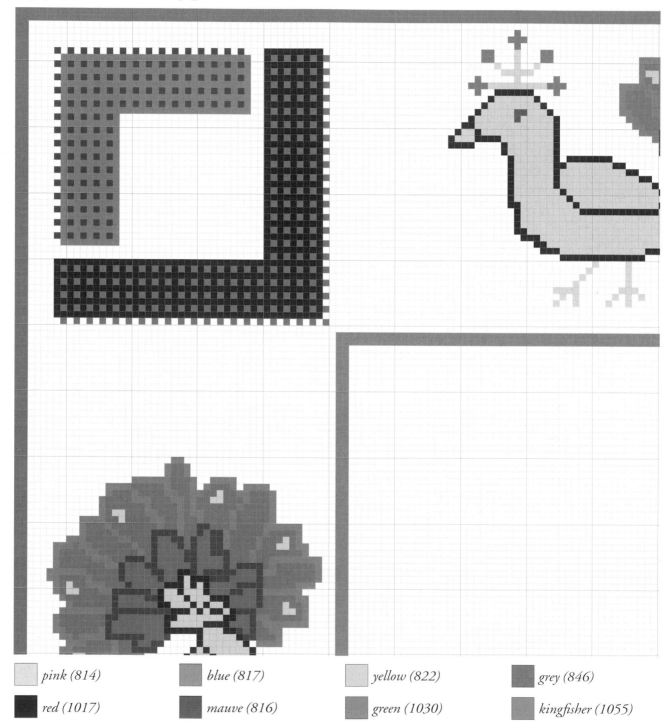

pink (814)	blue (817)	yellow (822)	grey (846)
red (1017)	mauve (816)	green (1030)	kingfisher (1055)

Top right of chart, continued on page 119

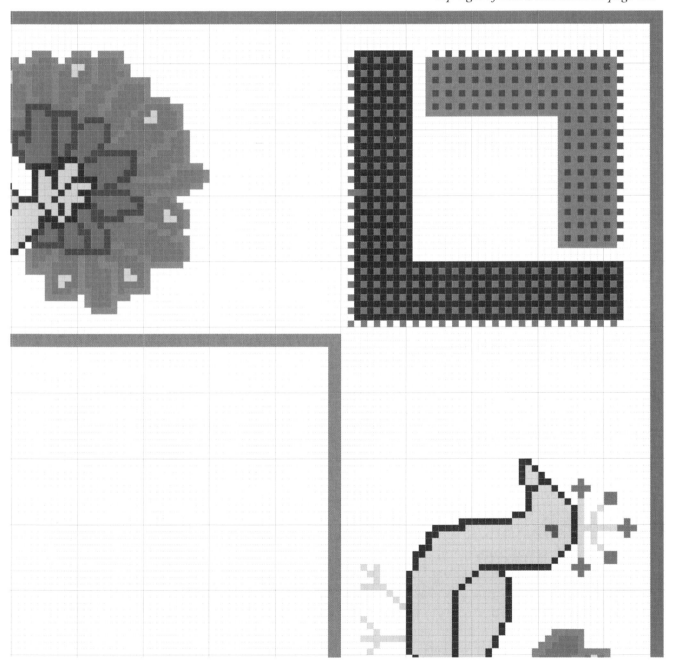

Bottom left of chart, continued from page 116

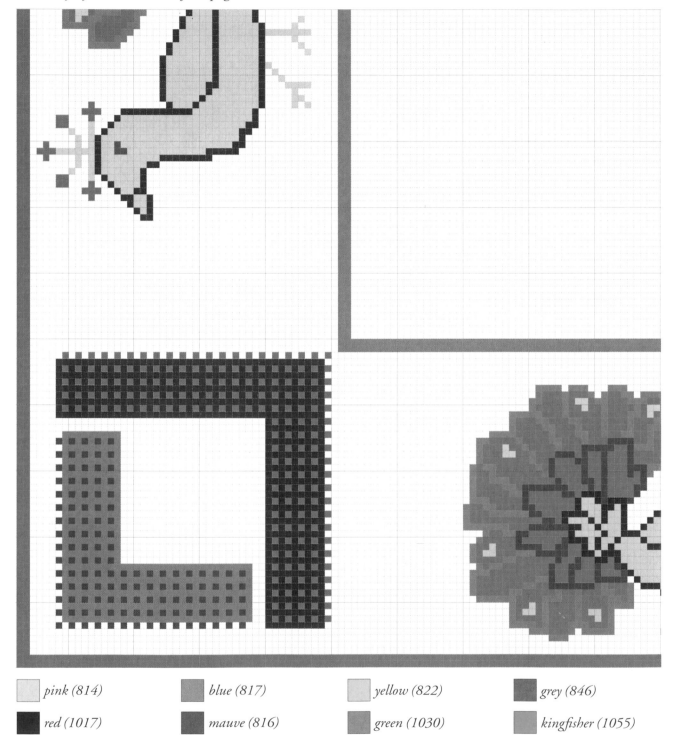

	pink (814)		blue (817)		yellow (822)		grey (846)
	red (1017)		mauve (816)		green (1030)		kingfisher (1055)

Bottom right of chart, continued from page 117

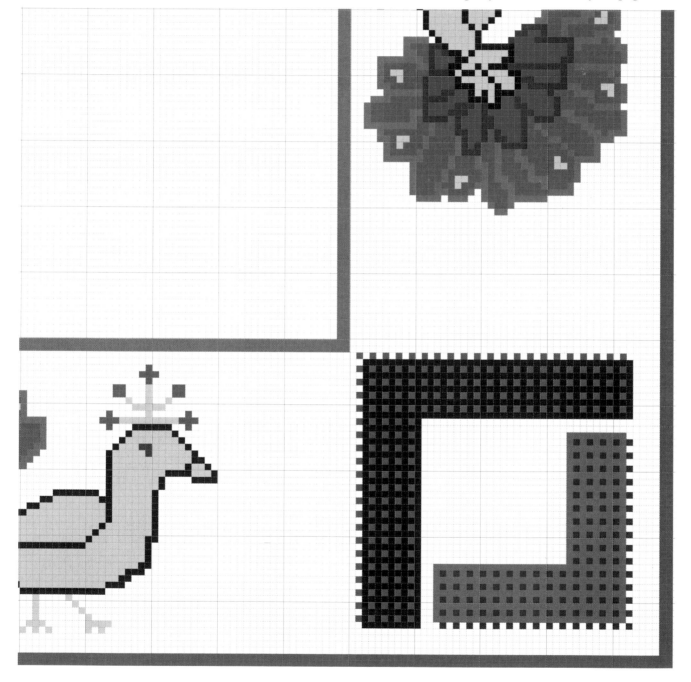

Two Jungle Beasts

INDIAN ELEPHANT

This most sacred fellow has a home-made frame covered in fabric. You could have great fun with the frame, painting it with fabric paints or adding shells and beads.

Actual design measures:
4¾ in (12 cm) square

MATERIALS

1 piece of 14-count Aida in black measuring 8 in (20 cm) square
No. 22 tapestry needle
2 pieces of card measuring 8½ in (21.5 cm) square
Craft knife
Glue (rubber cement)
1 piece of wadding (synthetic batting) measuring 8½ in (21.5 cm) square
1 piece of fabric (for covering the frame) measuring 10 in (25.5 cm) square
Self-adhesive picture hook or card for strut

Anchor Marlitt Threads:
1 skein of red (893)
1 skein of pink (814)
1 skein of green (1030)
1 skein of yellow (822)
1 skein of grey (870)

INSTRUCTIONS

Mark the centre of the chart and the centre of the fabric. Starting here, work in cross stitch using two strands of Marlitt. When the design is complete, press it on the wrong side over a damp cloth, face down on a soft towel.

Take one of the pieces of card and, with the craft knife, cut a 5½ in (14 cm) square from the centre. Do the same with the wadding (batting) and then glue it onto the front of the frame. Stretch your fabric over the padded frame

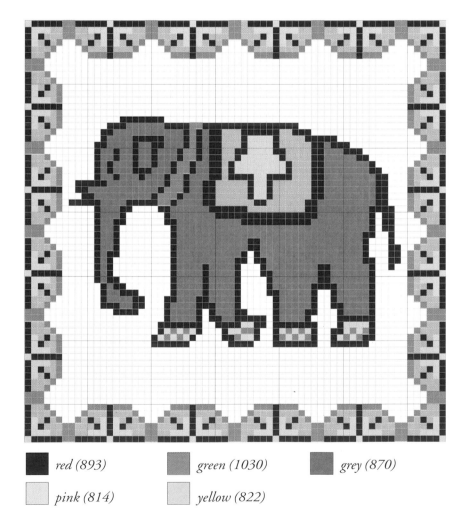

■	red (893)	▨	green (1030)	▨	grey (870)
▢	pink (814)	▨	yellow (822)		

and glue the raw outside edges to the back.

Make cuts from the centre of the fabric to each inside corner of the frame. Fold the fabric to the back of the card, then stretch it, trim the excess and glue into place. Now glue the cross-stitched Aida to the centre of the remaining piece of card putting the glue only on the outer edges. Leave to dry and then glue the frame firmly on top of the mounted cross stitch. Attach the self-adhesive hook to the back of the backing card.

INDIAN LION

The lion is a popular motif appearing on Indian textiles and is usually worked in chain stitch. I took him from a door hanging that lives in my kitchen. He is a companion piece to the Elephant which also appears in this section on pages 120-2.

Actual design measures:
4¾ in (12 cm) square

MATERIALS

1 piece of 14-count Aida in black measuring 8 in (20 cm) square

No. 22 tapestry needle

2 pieces of card measuring 8½ in (21.5 cm) square

Craft knife

Glue (rubber cement)

1 piece of wadding (synthetic batting) measuring 8½ in (21.5 cm) square

1 piece of fabric (for covering the frame) measuring 10 in (25.5 cm) square
Self-adhesive picture hook or card for strut

Anchor Marlitt Threads:
1 skein of yellow (822)
1 skein of red (893)
1 skein of green (1030)
1 skein of purple (817)
1 skein of dark grey (846)

INSTRUCTIONS

Mark the centre of the chart and the centre of the fabric. Starting here, work in cross stitch using two strands of Marlitt. When the design is complete, press it on the wrong side over a damp cloth, face down on a soft towel.

Take one of the pieces of card and, with the craft knife, cut a 5½ in (14 cm) square from the centre. Do the same with the wadding (batting) and then glue it onto the front of the frame. Stretch your fabric over the padded frame and glue the raw outside edges to the back.

Make cuts from the centre of the fabric to each inside corner of the frame. Fold the fabric to the back of the card, then stretch it, trim the excess and glue into place. Now glue the cross-stitched Aida to the centre of the remaining piece of card putting the glue only on the outer edges. Leave to dry and then glue the frame firmly on top of the mounted cross stitch. Attach the self-adhesive hook to the back of the backing card.

yellow (822)

red (893)

green (1030)

purple (817)

dark grey (846)

PENCIL HOLDER
WALLHANGING

This project was inspired by a small bag traditionally embroidered by a bride for her groom. Here the image is mounted on red felt and designed to hang on the wall, near the phone, to hold your pencils.

Actual design measures:
5¾ × 2¼ in (14.5 × 6 cm)

MATERIALS
1 piece of 14-count Aida in black measuring 7 × 4½ in (18 × 11.5 cm)
No. 22 tapestry needle
1 piece of red felt measuring 3 × 11 in (7.5 × 28 cm)
Sewing thread (to match the Aida)
4 pre-drilled shells

DMC Embroidery Cottons (floss):
1 skein of red (349)
1 skein of orange (740)
1 skein of ecru (822)
1 skein of yellow (742)

INSTRUCTIONS
Mark the centre of the chart and the centre of the fabric. Starting here, work in cross stitch using two strands of cotton (floss). When the design is complete, press it on the wrong side over a damp cloth, face down on a soft towel.

Fold under and trim the top two corners of the Aida two holes away from the design and hem into position. Take the felt and make a 1 in (2.5 cm)-wide hem at one short end (this will be the top). Leaving a 1½ in (4 cm)-wide border of felt at the bottom edge, and a ¼ in (5 mm)-wide border at the sides, fold under the raw side and bottom edges of the Aida and stitch the panel to the felt along the straight edges. Leave the top open.

To make the tassels, take five 8 in (20 cm) lengths of stranded cotton (floss), fold in half and bind at the top. Make four of these tassels and stitch them onto the bottom edge of the Aida. Sew the shells into position over the top loops of the tassels.

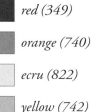

red (349)

orange (740)

ecru (822)

yellow (742)

SUN MOTIF POT LID

This design, featuring the popular sun motif, was inspired by an Afghanistan bedspread with a similar appliquéd motif. Framecraft (see Stockists on page 156) make a lovely selection of pots in numerous sizes and finishes which you can use to mount your finished cross-stitch pieces.

Actual design measures: 3 in (7.5 cm) diameter

MATERIALS

1 piece of 14-count Aida in black measuring 6 in (15 cm) square
No. 22 tapestry needle
1 circular pot with 4 in (10 cm)-diameter work space

DMC Embroidery Cottons (floss):

1 skein of mauve (208)
1 skein of ecru (822)
1 skein of red (349)
1 skein of gold (742)
1 skein of orange (740)

INSTRUCTIONS

Mark the centre of the chart and the centre of the fabric. Starting here, work in cross stitch using two strands of cotton (floss). When the design is complete, press it on the wrong side over a damp cloth, face down on a soft towel.

Place the design in the top of the pot, according to the manufacturer's instructions.

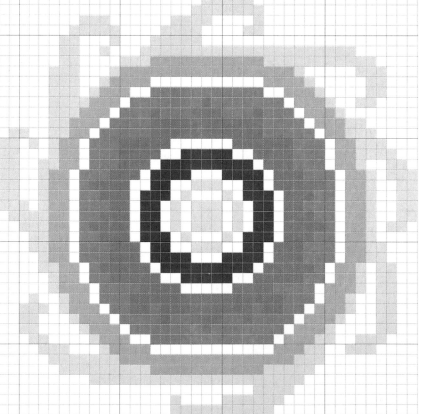

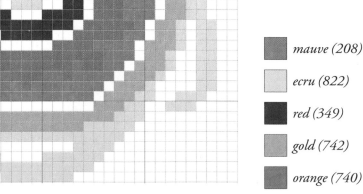

mauve (208)

ecru (822)

red (349)

gold (742)

orange (740)

EMBROIDERED DRESS

Plain dresses, be they kaftans or little black numbers, are a perfect background for your cross-stitch skills. Here, I have charted out the designs that appeared on a traditional Palestinian dress for you to use as you will. Since it is unlikely that you will have a dress of exactly the same shape/dimensions, I have not included thread quantities. But I have listed the closest colours I could find to the original worked piece. Since the pattern is made up from a series of repeating images, you can adjust the chart to fit the area you wish to cover.

MATERIALS
Paper for pattern
Felt-tipped pen
1 piece of 14-count waste canvas
    1½ in (4 cm) larger than the
    area you wish to embroider
No. 8 crewel needle
Tweezers

DMC Embroidery
Cottons (floss):
Chestnut (920)
Gold (783)
Red (326)
Cream (677)
Pale olive (834)
Coffee (3828)

Pale blue (798)
Blue (333)

THE YOKE
Actual design (half the yoke) measures (from the highest point of the shoulder to the bottom of the line of border stitches): 12½ × 6 in (32 × 15 cm)

INSTRUCTIONS
Lay the paper on your dress and draw an outline of the area you wish to cover, bearing in mind the shape of the charted yoke. Cut out a template from the paper and lay this on the waste canvas and draw around the outline onto the canvas. Cut the canvas leaving 1½ in (4 cm) around the edge of your drawn line.

Tack (baste) the canvas into position on the dress front. Begin working your cross stitch using 2 strands of cotton (floss) and starting at the centre of the neckline. Leave out areas of pattern to suit the shape of the neckline until the neck and shoulder patterns are complete. Work one half of the yoke first and then the other side.

When the design is complete, carefully remove the tacking (basting) thread and pull out the

strands of waste canvas from under the embroidery with tweezers. Press the yolk on the wrong side over a damp cloth, face down on a soft towel.

THE SQUARE PANELS
Actual design measures: 2 × 3 in (5 × 7.5 cm)

INSTRUCTIONS
These panels are positioned beneath the yoke and worked in cross stitch with the exception of the inverted V-shapes which are worked in back stitch. Tack (baste) your waste canvas into position and work the cross-stitched areas. Remove the tacking (basting) and the strands of canvas as before, and then work the lines of backstitch directly onto the fabric. Press when finished.

THE SLEEVES
Pattern as printed measures: 10¾ × 2¾ in (27 × 7 cm)

Three complete lozenge motifs measure: 2 in (5 cm) wide

INSTRUCTIONS
Calculate the diameter of the sleeve and the number of lozenges that will fit around it. Tack (baste) the

THE YOKE
Top left of chart, continues on page 132

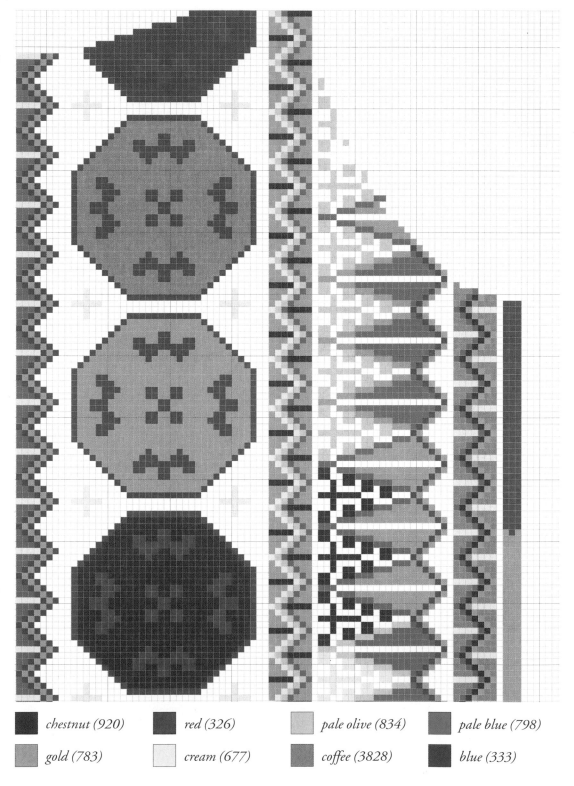

| | chestnut (920) | | red (326) | | pale olive (834) | | pale blue (798) |
| | gold (783) | | cream (677) | | coffee (3828) | | blue (333) |

THE YOKE
*Top right of
chart, continues
on page 133*

THE YOKE
AND THE
SQUARE
PANELS
*Bottom left of
chart, continued
from page 130*

| | chestnut (920) | | red (326) | | pale olive (834) | | pale blue (798) |
| | gold (783) | | cream (677) | | coffee (3828) | | blue (333) |

THE YOKE
AND THE
SQUARE
PANELS
*Bottom right of
chart, continued
from page 131*

THE SLEEVES

waste canvas into position and work the design as described above, starting at a centre lozenge placed at the centre front of your sleeve. Finish as close as you can to the sleeve seam on a complete lozenge and remove the waste canvas strands as before.

On the charts on this page, I have given you the pattern for the strips of design above and below the lozenge pattern (see the photograph opposite) together with some variations for the decorative narrow bands.

If you wish to cover the sleeve with a design, mix and match the sections of patterns given opposite, calculating the measurements from the completed yoke.

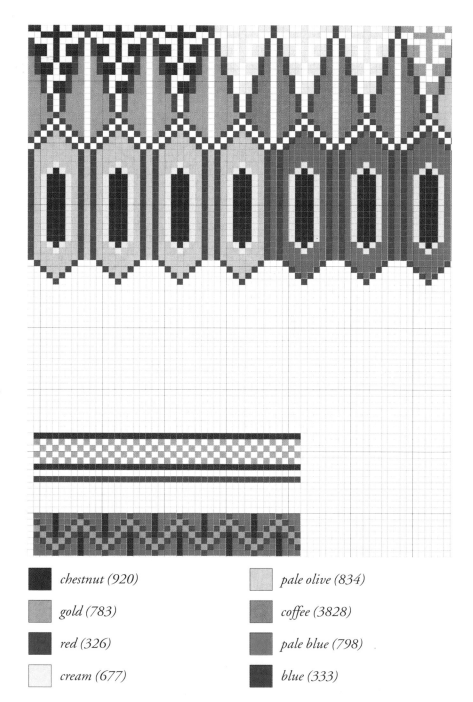

■	chestnut (920)	▢	pale olive (834)
▨	gold (783)	▨	coffee (3828)
▨	red (326)	▨	pale blue (798)
▢	cream (677)	■	blue (333)

Detail of the embroidered dress showing the sleeve. Stitch the lozenge design first and then add further strips of embroidery, selecting patterns from the chart opposite.

Satin Spectacles Case

H ere is a way to use a section of the dress design featured on pages 128-35 as a panel for the back of a spectacles case. The one here has a quilted black satin front which will provide a comfy home for your spectacles.

Actual design measures:
8½ × 3¾ in (21.5 × 9.5 cm)

MATERIALS
1 piece of 14-count Aida in black measuring 12½ × 8 in (32 × 20 cm)
No. 22 tapestry needle

1 piece of lining fabric measuring 10½ × 6 in (26.5 × 15 cm)
Cotton thread (to match the Aida)
1 piece of padded or quilted fabric measuring 9 × 6 in (22.5 × 15 cm)
1 piece of black edging braid measuring 22 in (56 cm)
1 press stud or velcro pad

DMC Embroidery Cottons (floss):

1 skein of chestnut (920)
1 skein of gold (783)
1 skein of red (326)
1 skein of coffee (3828)
1 skein of cream (677)
1 skein of pale olive (834)
1 skein of blue (798)

INSTRUCTIONS

Mark the centre of the chart and the centre of the Aida. Starting here, work in cross stitch using three strands of cotton (floss). When the design is complete, press it on the wrong side over a damp cloth, face down on a soft towel.

Cut the lining fabric to fit. Then turn in the raw edges of both the lining and the Aida and stitch together around the outer edge to form the back of the case. Line the piece of padded fabric in the same way to form the front of the case.

Pin the back and front together with wrong sides facing and sandwiching the braid along the side and bottom seams. Top sew these seams together.

Stitch one half of the press stud or velcro pad at the centre top of the lining on the overlap. Position and stitch the other half to match on the quilted fabric.

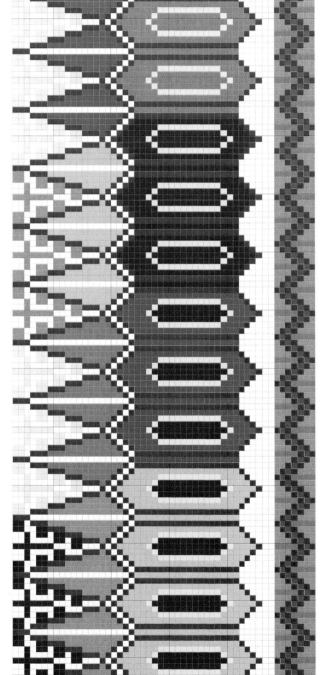

chestnut (920)

gold (783)

red (326)

coffee (3828)

cream (677)

pale olive (834)

blue (798)

SILK EVENING BAG

Make up this pretty evening bag to coordinate with your dress by picking out one of the dress's colours and using it in the cross-stitch design. The small brass rings we have used are the type sold for making eyelets, but key rings would work equally well.

Actual design measures:
16 × 3½ in (40.5 × 9 cm)

MATERIALS
1 piece of Aida 14-count fabric in black measuring 20 × 7½ in (51 × 19 cm)
No. 22 tapestry needle
1 piece of silk (or heavy cotton) fabric measuring 10 × 20 in (25.5 × 51 cm)
2 pieces of same measuring 6 in (15 cm) square
Cotton thread (to match the silk fabric)
Sewing needle
1 piece of card cut in a circle measuring 5 in (13 cm) in diameter
1 length of cord measuring 1 yd (1 m)
Small brass rings

DMC Embroidery Cottons (floss):
1 skein of chestnut (920)
1 skein of gold (783)
1 skein of red (326)
1 skein of coffee (3828)
1 skein of blue (333)
1 skein of cream (677)
1 skein of pale olive (834)
1 skein of pale blue (798)

INSTRUCTIONS
Mark the centre of the chart and the centre of the Aida. Starting here, work in cross stitch using two strands of cotton (floss). When the design is complete, press it on the wrong side over a damp cloth, face down on a soft towel.

Take the strip of silk fabric and make a 1 in (2.5 cm)-wide hem along one long edge. Stitch the other long edge to the top of the cross stitch, turning in raw edges of both fabric and Aida.

Stitch the short ends together to form a tube. Next, place the circle of card between the two remaining squares of fabric and stitch all around the circle. Trim off the corners of the fabric so that you have a 1 in (2.5 cm) circular selvedge. Insert this base into the bottom of the tube and hand-sew it to the bottom of the cross stitch, turning in all raw edges. Stitch on the brass rings, approximately 1 in (2.5 cm) below the top hem, spacing them evenly. Thread the cord through the rings and tie in a bow.

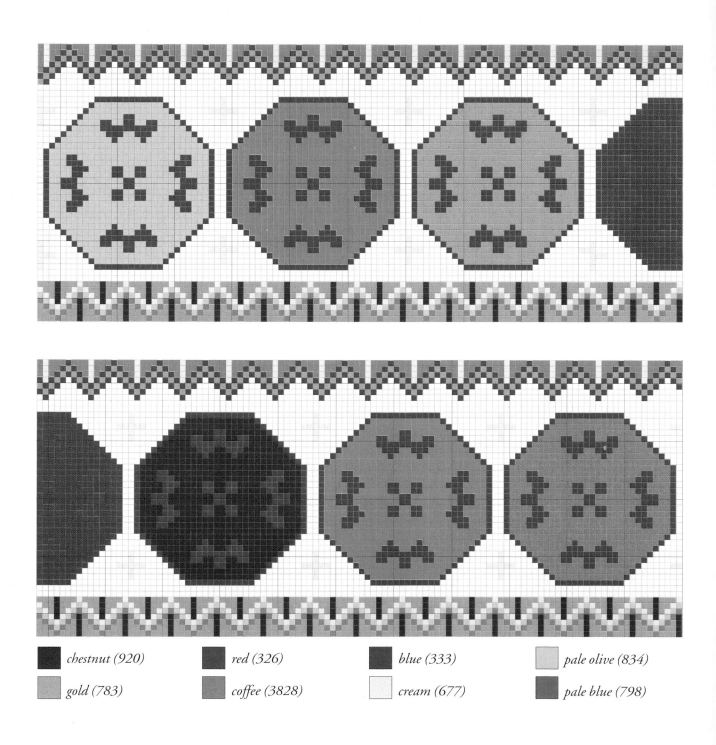

chestnut (920)

red (326)

blue (333)

pale olive (834)

gold (783)

coffee (3828)

cream (677)

pale blue (798)

EMBROIDERED LINEN TOP

With the help of waste canvas you can decorate any plain shirt with cross-stitch motifs. Because this one had a tiny mark on it, I bought it cheaply from a popular retail chain store. The mark is now neatly hidden behind the cross-stitched motif.

Actual design measures:
Small spot motifs
1 in (2.5 cm) square
Neckband motif
½ in (1 cm) deep
Sleeve motif
5½ × 1½ in (14 × 4 cm)

MATERIALS

10 pieces of 14-count waste canvas measuring 2 in (5 cm) square
2 pieces of same measuring 7 × 2 in (18 × 5 cm)
1 piece of same to fit over neckband length
No. 8 crewel needle
Tweezers
Thread (to match garment)

DMC Embroidery Cottons (floss):
1 skein of dark rose (3722)
1 skein of rose (224)
1 skein of pale rose (893)

INSTRUCTIONS

Lay out the shirt and arrange the squares of waste canvas on the front, spacing them evenly. Tack (baste) them into position around the outer edge of each square. Position the pieces for the sleeve motifs if required, and then stitch on the final piece for the neckband. Mark the centre of each chart and the centre of the pieces of canvas.

Starting here, work in cross stitch using two strands of cotton (floss). When working the neckband, repeat the design until you have your required length. When the designs are complete, carefully remove the tacking (basting) stitches, then pull the strands of waste canvas from under the embroidery using tweezers. Press the finished pieces on the wrong side over a damp cloth, face down on a soft towel.

■ *dark rose (3722)*   ■ *rose (224)*   ■ *pale rose (893)*

CAMEL HATBAND

Finished bands of embroidery fabric are now available ready-made with a selection of trims and in various counts. This gives you the opportunity to embroider cake bands, shelf trims or a hat band like this one, which has been inspired by Palestinian motifs.

Actual design measures: 5¾ × 2½ in (14.5 × 6.5 cm)

MATERIALS

1 length of 14-count Aida in white with pink trim measuring 25 × 3½ in (63.5 × 9 cm)
Cotton thread (white)
No. 22 tapestry needle
White straw hat

DMC Embroidery Cottons (floss):

1 skein of dark rose (3722)
1 skein of rose (224)
1 skein of pale rose (893)

INSTRUCTIONS

Using the sewing thread, make a ½ in (1 cm)-wide hem at each end of the fabric band. Starting ½ in (1 cm) in from the fold on the hemmed edge, work the design in cross stitch using three strands of cotton (floss). Leaving 3 in (7.5 cm) between each pattern, repeat three times more. When the design is complete, press it on the wrong side over a damp cloth, face down on a soft towel.

Lay the band around the hat crossing the ends at the back. Secure the crossed section on to the hat with a couple of stitches.

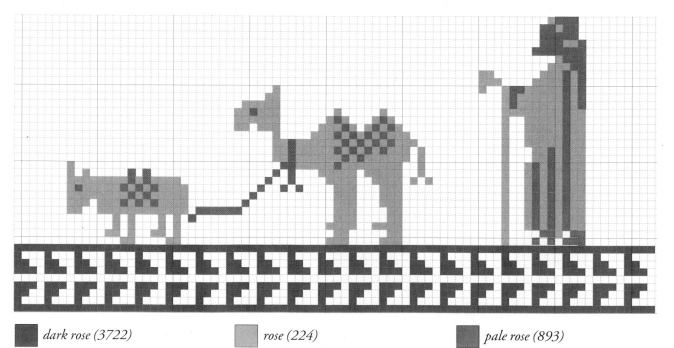

■ *dark rose (3722)*   ■ *rose (224)*   ■ *pale rose (893)*

TECHNIQUES

Cross stitch should be a relaxing and therapeutic pastime. For this reason I have no intention of challenging you with complicated instructions or baffling you with brilliant finishing techniques. The object of the exercise is simply to achieve a neatly worked piece of embroidery without bumps and blemishes and to ensure that all your top stitches slope in the same direction. Alongside each project, I have indicated my own approach to making up the specific items. There are many other ways of achieving the same results and it really doesn't matter what route you take, so long as you are happy with your finished piece of work.

The following information in this section will introduce you to the variety of materials and techniques that you can use in order to transform your design into something special. These materials and guidelines are tried and tested and are those 'rules' that give you the means to produce a truly professionally finished piece of work each time you pick up your embroidery thread and a needle.

TOOLBOX

If you are a newcomer to cross stitch, fill your work box with the following items:

Evenweave and plainweave fabric offcuts (see Fabric Matters, overleaf)

Assorted cotton threads

Crewel needles (those with large eyes and sharp points)

Tapestry needles (those with large eyes and blunt points)

Sharp scissors

Waste canvas (see Fabric Matters, page 149)

Embroidery frame (optional)

Pencils (plain and transfer)

Tracing paper

Tape measure

Assorted backing fabrics

Wadding (synthetic batting)

Ribbons and laces for trimming

Rubber-based adhesive

Clear adhesive

Medium-weight card

FABRIC MATTERS

The first thing you must decide is which material you are going to stitch on. This will be dictated by the size and purpose of your finished item, the intricacy of the design, and your chosen threads. I have listed here a selection of traditional needlework fabrics, all of which should be available in any good needlecraft shop.

Several fabrics are produced especially for cross stitch and make life easier for you as the holes in which you stitch are clearly defined. These are great for beginners. In this category I would recommend Aida or Binca. These are brand names for basketweave fabrics which are available in a range of different counts (stitches per inch), and will enable you to produce a bold, striking pattern or delicate, intricate design with relative ease.

The count you select will determine the size of your finished embroidery and will also dictate the thickness of the thread that you can use. The lower the count of the fabric, the less stitches per inch it will produce and the larger your design will appear. Binca is widely used in schools and for children's projects because the count is around 6 stitches per inch and it is available in a good range of bright colours. Aida, on the other hand, is usually available in 11-18 count in a more subtle range of colours. DMC have recently introduced Aida Plus which is a coated Aida that can be cut without fraying and is useful for items that require a stiff base.

In addition to traditional evenweave fabrics, manufacturers are now extending their ranges to include damasks with inserted evenweave panels ready for you to embroider. You can also find special Aida and linen borders to embroider and stitch onto towels and bedspreads for example.

Evenweave Fabrics
Needlecraft shops stock a wide range of what are known as evenweave fabrics. 'Evenweave' means that there is an equal number of horizontal and vertical threads to the inch, making it easy to count the holes and to make your stitches a uniform size. Once again, select your fabric according to the count, which is, in this case, determined by the number of threads that you work your crosses over when making a stitch.

For example, for fine work you would choose a fabric with a high count and work over one or two threads, while for a bold pattern you would choose a coarser fabric and decide how big you wanted your stitches to be by determining how many threads you were going to work over. Throughout the text in this book I have referred to the measurement of the canvas as holes per inch, which is exactly as it seems. Place your measure on a vertical thread of canvas and count how many holes you get in the row for 1 in (2.5 cm).

Hardanger and Linda are both attractive evenweave fabrics that can be bought from good needlework stores. Jobelan is available in a huge range of colours that will make a lovely background for your designs.

Embroidery linens can be purchased in high counts and provide you with a sophisticated background for your work. However, they are expensive, and before selecting them give consideration to your sight and the time available to you. If you have owlish vision and endless time on your hands you could produce cross-stitch miniatures by working on silk gauze; this can be purchased pre-mounted in a card

frame but really needs to be worked through a magnifying glass: eat lots of carrots before you begin.

A relative newcomer to embroidery materials is plastic canvas. It is particularly popular with children, has various high counts, and can be used for three-dimensional projects such as boxes and toys. Plastic canvas is fun to work with and your projects will be completed quickly.

Paper canvas is a traditional medium which reached its height of popularity during the Victorian era. It is currently enjoying a revival among stitchers and is used for cut-outs (see Two Jabirus and a Spoonbill on pages 110-11) and also for various items such as greetings cards, bookmarks and Christmas decorations.

Canvas
Canvas is normally associated with needlepoint rather than cross stitch because it is a coarse, stiff evenweave fabric with clearly defined holes.

Standard needlepoint canvases consist of an interlocked single thread (mono canvas) or interlocked double threads (double or Penelope canvas). Both varieties are available in a number of different counts, although from 10-count downwards, you should work with wool rather than cotton.

Waste not
Waste canvas is a miraculous invention that makes it possible for you to work on a vast range of fabrics. It is basically a very loosely woven canvas that is available in a selection of counts. The method is that you tack (baste) the canvas onto your fabric so that it forms an instant grid that defines the size and position of your stitches to the same extent as Aida. Cross stitch your design in the normal way and then pull out the threads of waste canvas from underneath your embroidery with the help of a pair of tweezers. If you pull out all the vertical threads first you will find that the horizontal threads virtually fall away by themselves. If you have any problem removing these threads, dampen the fabric and you will find they are easier to remove.

Specialist Embroidery Fabrics
These are usually sold by the yard (metre), although you will often require only a very small piece for a project such as a greeting card. For this reason, many needlecraft shops sell bags of mixed off-cuts, which really can prove to be good value.

Buyer Beware
Any fabric shop will offer you a vast range of delights on which to embroider designs, but most general fabrics are plainweave and often impossible to 'count'. With a little experience you can safely select cottons with regular patterning such as stripes, ginghams and damasks and gauge your stitch positions according to the printed pattern. Do not attempt to use stretchy or knitted fabrics — your work may pucker. Once again, you must take into account the thickness and the weight of the threads you intend to use before you select your background material.

GLORIOUS THREADS
With the exception of projects in the Treasures from Afar section I have worked all my designs using DMC threads. While I have specified particular colours, your finished effect will not be spoilt if you go up or down a shade.

Stranded cottons (floss) go a long way, especially if you are working on a high count fabric, so, after cross stitching for just a short time, you are bound to build up a useful collection of ends of skeins that can be incorporated into future projects.

There are a vast array of threads on the market and your choice will add to the individuality of your work. I have listed a selection of these below and leave it to you to experiment with the different effects and highlights that you can achieve with them.

A major consideration should be that all the threads you use in a single project should be of the same thickness. If you mix thicknesses, you will end up with some skimpy crosses and some fat ones which will not be a pretty sight unless, of course, you intend them to look that way.

Stranded Cottons (floss)
These are sold in small 8m (approximately 26ft) skeins containing six individual threads. The idea is that you cut a workable length (say, 20 in [51 cm]) and separate the threads so that you have as many strands as you need for your particular canvas. You can, of course, mix together strands of several colours to give a subtle

shaded effect and you can buy skeins that are already shaded. You might, in your future discussions as a serious embroiderer, hear the word 'floss', this describes one single strand of thread.

Coton à Broder

This is a flat, unmercerized thread which works well in bolder designs. It comes in a good range of colours but does pick up the dust more easily than the slightly shiny varieties. Danish and German flower threads are also flat cottons but are finer. All of the above threads are spun as a single thread and are not designed to be separated or stranded. They impart a lovely soft quality to your work.

Silks

Stranded cottons (floss) are mercerized and therefore have a silky lustre. However, for the perfectionists among us, there is nothing like the real thing. Silk is available in stranded form and in twisted threads. Unfortunately, it is expensive and not very easy to work with because the delicate fibres tend to snag on rough skin. However, the finished effect on very fine work is quite special... reserve it for your masterpiece.

Pearl Cottons

Pearl cotton (coton perlé) is a single twisted, high lustre thread that comes in a good selection of colours including some with a shaded effect. These cottons are available in three different weights which you should select according to your back-ground fabric.

Marlitt

This is a synthetic thread with a high sheen. It is very effective and a good substitute for silk. Marlitt is an Anchor thread.

Fancies

In addition to the above, fancy threads, including a wonderful range of metallics by Kreinik, are constantly being introduced onto the market. These can be used to especially great effect for highlighting details, but be sure to check that the thickness of the thread will marry with the basic threads you have chosen.

Get Organized

If you are anything like me, you will always pull the wrong loose end on a skein of cotton (floss) and end up with a knotted mess that will prove a great joy to your cat. To avoid this, it is a good idea to make yourself a thread organizer before beginning a project. All you need is a small strip of light-weight card (an old greetings card is ideal) and a hole punch. Make a hole for each colour down the right-hand side of the card and cut your thread into manageable lengths – say, 20 in (51 cm). Write the colour number and, if appropriate, the symbol on the chart, next to a punched hole and loop your lengths of thread through it. You can then easily pull out the thread as and when you need it.

NEEDLE TALK

For cross stitch on evenweave fabric or linen, you need a selection of crewel needles. These have a sharp point and long, flat eyes so that you can thread through a number of strands at a time without damaging the fabric when you push the needle through. Crewel needles are available in a number of different sizes, and the size you select will depend on the number of threads you are intending to use.

A suggested size is given with each project in this book but, as a rule of thumb, work with a needle that feels comfortable, threads easily and travels smoothly through your fabric.

EMBROIDERY FRAMES

When I am working with an evenweave fabric such as Aida, I do not consider it necessary to use a frame. However, I always use a frame when I am stitching on plainweave fabrics or working on a very large project.

There are various types of frames on the market although the most popular kind for cross stitch is the hoop, which consists of two concentric circles, one of which is laid under your work and the other laid over your work and then tightened with a screw to hold the fabric taut. It is a good idea to bind both rings with masking tape before beginning because the hoop may mark or distort delicate fabrics. Always remove your work from the hoop at the end of a stitching session.

The second most popular type of frame consists of two parallel dowels with webbing onto which you tack (baste) the opposite ends of your fabric. The dowels are then slotted into two straight uprights, which can be tightened with wing nuts to hold the dowels securely. You can then rotate the dowels to move the fabric up and down and keep it taut.

LET THERE BE LIGHT

One miracle of modern science that I would not be without is the daylight bulb. Given that most of us are busy people who only have the evenings available to stitch in, good lighting, especially when you are counting stitches, is essential. Daylight bulbs ease the strain and can be combined with a custom-made magnifying lamp on an anglepoise-type stand which makes stitching comfortable and pleasurable (see Stockists on page 156). You can also buy special holders for your charts and no end of other paraphernalia that will help you to get the job done and take any potential strain out of your work.

CHARTS

Many people are frightened of charts which really need not be the case. All you have to do is to remember that every coloured square represents one complete stitch. The heavier lines on the grid are put there to make counting easier for you, as each block of squares between the heavy lines represents ten stitches. Your colour key gives you the correct colour-coded thread to use so you really cannot go wrong.

If you find that you get lost on a chart, the best solution is to take a photocopy of it and to cross off the squares as you work them. I work in blocks of colour rather than rows and I keep a number of needles threaded up with the different shades so I can chop and change as and when it becomes necessary.

SIZING THE DESIGN

For each of the designs in this book I give the actual size of the motif that you will achieve if you work on my recommended background fabric. However, it is quite easy to re-size the motif by changing the count of the fabric you use. There is a simple formula for working out the size of your design; let's take the Fleur-de-lis Box Top design on pages 49-51 as an example.

First, count the number of stitches across the chart at the widest point; on this chart it is 90 stitches. Now count the number of stitches vertically; it is 87. If you were going to work this design on 28-count linen over two threads, you would need to halve the count to determine the number of stitches to the inch. On 28-count linen you would achieve 14 stitches to the inch. You should now divide the number of stitches on your chart by the number of stitches to the inch.

In this case, then, the width of 90 stitches is divided by 14 to give you 6.42in (approximately 16.5 cm). The height of 87 stitches when divided by 14 gives you 6.21in (approximately 16 cm).

When you are working on Aida or over one thread of fabric, there is no need to halve the count before dividing. When calculating how much fabric you require you should also remember to add at least 1 in (2.5 cm) of extra fabric on all sides of each project to allow for backing or, if it is a picture, 2 in (5 cm) for mounting.

If you want to re-size a design in a major way, your best approach is with a hand-drawn grid. First, trace the outline of your design and draw a squared grid over it. Draw a second grid to the size you require and copy the design square by square from one to the other. Place the enlarged version over a sheet of graph paper and fill in symbols within the traced outlines.

Charting paper is now available in clear acetate and you can place this over any image that you wish to chart and fill in the symbols. Alternatively, you can enlarge your design with the use of a photocopier and then re-define the grid by drawing in extra crossed lines to fill in with symbols.

Yet another method of enlarging is to read every symbol on the chart as a block of four stitches. In principle, this will double the size of your design although you may find it necessary to round off corners by taking away or adding a few stitches at the edges as you are working.

Transferring designs

If you do not wish to work with waste canvas, you can easily transfer the image with a water-erasable transfer pencil (these are available from needlework shops and haberdashers) and some tracing paper. First, test your fabric by drawing a cross on the tracing paper. Place this face down on the fabric and press it with a warm iron. If this takes to the fabric, you can then trace your complete design and transfer it. There are some wonderful colour transfer pens and paints on the market, so you could trace or paint the design in full colour and then transfer it to the fabric by ironing.

Centring designs

Throughout the book I have suggested that you find the centre of the fabric before beginning your embroidery. There are various methods of doing this. If you are using Aida you can count the holes vertically and horizontally and halve the totals to find the centre. You could use a tape measure and halve the measurement, or you can fold your fabric both horizontally and vertically to establish the centre point. When you are establishing the centre point on a piece of fabric that has more selvedge on one side or the other, start your count or measurement after the selvedge line.

To find the centre of the charts, count the stitches and halve the total. If there is no stitch at the centre point, count out to the nearest stitch and start on the equivalent position on your fabric.

On establishing your central point you might find it useful to tack (baste) a line of stitches, both horizontally and vertically, on your fabric as a guide. Always work out from the centre unless instructions specify otherwise.

READY, STEADY, GO

Before beginning your work, prevent potential disasters by making sure of the following:

1 Your hands are spotlessly clean and do not smell of garlic, cheese or cat. They will need regular washing as cotton picks up the dirt very easily.

2 Your tea or coffee is at a safe distance from your work and nothing tempting, like a chocolate bar or some peanut butter sandwiches, is nearby.

3 The animals have all been instructed not to sit on your lap/shoulder/head, and have learnt to wipe their paws before coming in from the garden and clambering all over you.

4 The children are well occupied and safe.

5 No one or nothing within reach of you is moulting.

STITCHING

Remember the first rule of cross stitch — that all the top stitches slope in the same direction. This can be achieved either by working a row of bottom stitches in one direction and then coming back along the row in the opposite direction or by working each complete cross individually. Both

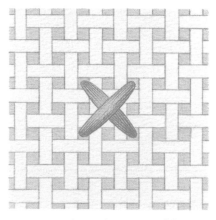

Cross stitch on plainweave fabric.

Cross stitch on evenweave fabric (Aida).

these methods are perfectly acceptable but the option you choose should depend on how many stitches you have in a row before the colour changes. You can work in any direction, but always insert your needle after the correct number of threads in your background material.

The diagrams, left, show a cross stitch worked over two threads on plainweave fabric and the position of your stitch on evenweave fabric.

It is a good idea to thread up several needles with different colours before you begin. Use a needle threader, it will save your sight and a great deal of time.

Cross stitch is the only stitch you need to master to complete the majority of projects in this book. However, one or two of the designs require additional stitches. When I refer to straight stitch I mean exactly that: small, back stitches worked in a row, the same size as a half cross stitch. Half stitch is as it sounds, work the first half of a cross stitch only, do not go back to complete the full cross.

STRETCHED OUT

I did not find it necessary to block any of the projects in this book. However, if you do find the shape of your work is slightly distorted, place it, face down on a sheet of blockboard, which you should cover with clean paper or a sheet. Then pull it into shape by inserting tacks along each edge at 1 in (2.5 cm) intervals. Dampen your work with a sponge or spray and leave it to dry.

FRAMING

Because cross-stitch fabric is very soft, when you are framing projects it is usually quite simple to stretch your finished work into shape on thick, acid-free backing board. Then either glue it into position using a rubber-based adhesive or use strong cotton thread to lace it across the back criss-cross fashion, until it is taut (see diagram, below).

Before using either of those methods, centre your finished work on your card and then insert pins into the edge of the needlework and card. Start with the four corners and then space them at 1 in (2.5 cm) intervals to ensure the fabric is straight and not distorted.

You can then add a decorative mount to the front or frame it in whatever fashion pleases you. Finished pieces intended for book covers and folders can be pulled into shape during the making-up process. When mounting a piece of embroidery, use acid-free card to ensure that it remains in good condition for the generations ahead of you who will hopefully treasure it.

TRIMMINGS

I hope this book has given you lots of new ideas for uses for your cross-stitch projects. Most crafty people are, by nature, collectors and I would expect you to have a basket or box of fabric oddments and furnishing trims. Use whatever you fancy to make up a project, but take into account the weight of any fabric you intend using against the weight of the material you have cross-stitched on.

In a couple of projects I have used twisted cords as an edging. To make a twisted cord, hold several strands of cotton (floss) together and tie one end to something solid like a door handle or a partner. Repeatedly twist this length of cotton (floss) until it is tight and then, keeping the twist, unfasten the tied end. Hold both ends together and let the doubled cotton twist around itself. Secure at both ends.

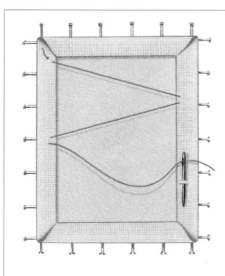 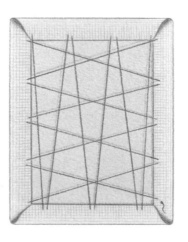

To frame your cross stitch, centre the finished work on a sheet of cardboard and insert pins all the way round at 1 in (2.5 cm) intervals. Then either glue it into position or lace across the back with string, as shown here.

I have also used simple tassels. To make these, take several lengths of thread and fold them in two. Repeatedly bind a thread around these just below the fold and secure by threading the end through the binding from top to bottom. Then trim the bottom edge into a straight line. Attach the tassels to your project by running a needle through the fold at the top of each tassel.

AFTERCARE

However careful you are, accidents inevitably happen. But, if you have used the recommended threads, you should have no problem repairing the damage. Before washing an embroidery, always check the colour fastness of the thread and fabric you have used and follow the manufacturer's instructions. DMC threads are reputed to be fast-dyed and can be machine washed at 95° F (35° C), but you must also take into account the instructions for washing the background fabric. As a general rule, always avoid bleach and biological powders and do not tumble dry. When you iron your work, place it face down over a fluffy towel to prevent flattening of the stitches. Then steam press or use a damp cloth, ironing on the wrong side of the work only.

STOCKISTS (SUPPLIERS) INFORMATION

Many of the lace and cotton items featured in this book are available as complete embroidery kits by mail order. For full details contact:

Melinda Coss
Ty'r Waun Bach
Gwernogle
Dyfed
West Wales SA32 7RY
United Kingdom
Telephone and fax:
(01267) 202386
(office hours only please)
email:
coss@cix.compulink.co.uk

For a selection of jars and other gift accessories for cross stitch contact:

Framecraft Miniatures Ltd
148-150 High Street
Aston
Birmingham B6 4US
England

Ann Brinkley Designs
761 Palmer Ave
Holmdel
NJ 97733
USA

Gay Bowles
PO Box 1060
Jannesville
WI 53547
USA

Threads and Fabrics

DMC Creative World Ltd
Pullman Road
Wigston
Leics LE18 2DY
England

DMC Import Kerny
Building 10
South Kerny
NJ 07032
USA

For Anchor cottons, Marlitt, Kreinik metallics, Aida fabrics and ready-to-sew accessories, contact:

Coats Patons Crafts
PO Box
McMullen Rd
Darlington
Co. Durham DL1 1YQ
England

Coats & Clark Inc
30 Patewood Drive
Suite 351
Greenville
S. Carolina 29615
USA

Kreinik Mfg. Co., Inc
9199 Reisterstown Rd
Suite 209B
Owings Mills
MD 21117
USA

Jobelan Fabrics
Fabric Flair
The Old Brewery
The Close
Warminster
Wilts BA12 9AL
England

Daylight bulbs and magnifying lamps are available from:

Daylight Studios
223a Portobello Rd
London W11 1LU
England

Transfer pens, paints, needlework fabrics and lots more available from:

Atlascraft Ltd
Ludlow Hill Road
Melton Rd
West Bridgford
Nottingham NG2 6HD
England

The cupboard for the Norwegian Warrior and the key plaque for the Norwegian Doves were made by David Tyler who will create similar items for you to your specifications:

David Tyler
Cwm Mawr Du
Gwernogle
Dyfed
West Wales SA32 7RN
United Kingdom

For details of ribbon stockists contact:

Offray Ribbon
Fir Tree Place
Church Rd
Ashford
Middx TW15 2PH
England

ACKNOWLEDGMENTS

Enormous amounts of gratitude are due to the following people for their superb help and support: for making this book possible through their excellent and endless stitching: Carol Edwards, Jane Fox, Lin Gensberg, Coral Gibson, Josie Hyde, Carolyn Palmer, Anne Peterson and Claire Powderly. For turning the needleworks into lovely things: Jeanette Hall. For their wonderful photography: Jon and Barbara Stewart. For moral support and daft ideas prevention: my editors, Cindy Richards, Jane Struthers and Emma Callery.

INDEX